ARTHURIAN TORSO

ARTHURIAN TORSO

CONTAINING THE POSTHUMOUS FRAGMENT OF

THE FIGURE OF ARTHUR

by

CHARLES WILLIAMS

AND

A COMMENTARY ON
THE ARTHURIAN POEMS OF
CHARLES WILLIAMS

by

C. S. LEWIS

Fellow of Magdalen College, Oxford

Geoffrey Cumberlege

OXFORD UNIVERSITY PRESS

London   New York   Toronto

Oxford University Press, Amen House, London, E.C.4

GLASGOW   NEW YORK   TORONTO   MELBOURNE   WELLINGTON
BOMBAY   CALCUTTA   MADRAS   CAPE TOWN
Geoffrey Cumberlege, Publisher to the University

First published   1948
Second impression 1952

Printed in Great Britain
by Jarrold & Sons Ltd., Norwich

To

MICHAL WILLIAMS

*without whose permission this book could not
have been made*

HEU QUIS TE CASUS DEIECTAM CONIUGE TANTO
EXCIPIT AUT QUAE DIGNA SATIS FORTUNA REVISIT,
HECTORIS ANDROMACHE?

CONTENTS

ACKNOWLEDGEMENTS

THE quotation from Charles Williams's novel *The Greater Trumps* are included by permission of Victor Gollancz Ltd. *Taliessin Through Logres* and *The Region of the Summer Stars* are published by the Oxford University Press. My thanks are due to Mrs. Hadfield for her kindness in putting at my disposal her typed copy of the MS. of *The Figure of Arthur*

—C. S. L.

INTRODUCTORY

W HEN Charles Williams died in 1945 he left two works unfinished. One was a long lyric cycle on the Arthurian legend of which two instalments had already appeared under the titles of *Taliessin through Logres* (1938) and *The Region of the Summer Stars* (1944). The other was a prose work on the history of the legend which was to have been entitled *The Figure of Arthur*.

The lyrical cycle is a difficult work which, if left without a commentary, might soon become another such battlefield for competing interpretations as Blake's *Prophetic Books*. Since I had heard nearly all of it read aloud and expounded by the author and had questioned him closely on his meaning I felt that I might be able to comment on it, though imperfectly, yet usefully. His most systematic exposition had been given to me in a long letter which (with that usual folly which forbids us to remember that our friends can die) I did not preserve ; but fortunately I had copied large extracts from it into the margin of my copy of *Taliessin* at the relevant passages. On these, and on memory and comparison with Williams's other works, I based a course of lectures on the cycle which I gave at Oxford in the autumn of 1945. Since a reasonable number of people appeared to be interested I then decided to make these lectures into a book.

It soon became clear that I could hardly explain the narrative assumptions of the cycle without giving some account of the earlier forms of the story—a heavy task which I shrank from undertaking. On the other hand, those to whom Williams had committed the manuscript of the unfinished *Figure of Arthur* were at the same time considering how that fragment could be most suitably published. The plan on which the present book has been arranged seemed to be the best solution of both problems. In it Williams the critic and literary historian provides

1

an introduction to my study of Williams the Arthurian poet ;
or, if you prefer, I add to Williams's history of the legend an
account of the last poet who has contributed to it—namely,
Williams himself. Chapters IV and V of his work I saw for the
first time when Mrs. A. M. Hadfield sent me a typed copy of
them. The two first chapters had been read aloud by the author
to Professor Tolkien and myself. It may help the reader to
imagine the scene ; or at least it is to me both great pleasure
and great pain to recall. Picture to yourself, then, an upstairs
sitting-room with windows looking north into the ' grove '
of Magdalen College on a sunshiny Monday Morning in vacation
at about ten o'clock. The Professor and I, both on the chester-
field, lit our pipes and stretched out our legs. Williams in the
arm-chair opposite to us threw his cigarette into the grate, took
up a pile of the extremely small, loose sheets on which he
habitually wrote—they came, I think, from a twopenny pad for
memoranda—and began as follows :—

THE FIGURE OF ARTHUR

by Charles Williams

CHAPTER I

The Beginnings

THE point at which the myth of Arthur begins does not, in its first appearance, hold any mention of the king. It does not, in fact, hold the name of a hero at all. It occurs in the pages of a treatise by a monk writing in the middle of the sixth century ; his name was Gildas, and the name of his book *De Excidio Britanniae*. The book is largely made up of exhortations to the Britons and of denunciations of their wicked kings, but these are preceded by a brief history of Britain since the coming of the Romans. He speaks of the withdrawal of the Romans, of the Saxon invasions, and of the wars between the Saxons and the Britons. The Britons were almost continuously defeated—many killed, some enslaved, some fugitives in the mountains or in exile beyond the sea—until they found a leader called Ambrosius Aurelianus. He was the descendant of a noble Roman family, but himself not notable until this crisis arose. He had some success against the Saxons, and established with them a kind of uncertain equality in the field. ' The battles ', says Gildas, ' were sometimes won by my countrymen and sometimes by the enemy.' This state of affairs lasted until the *obsessio Badonici montis*—the siege of Mount Badon. ' What was almost the last—though not the least—destruction of our cruel foes took place there.' Gildas adds that his own birth happened at this time. He mentions a period of forty-four years and one month, but scholars are divided whether this is meant to conclude in or begin from the battle. It would be convenient to the myth to suppose it the latter.

After the victory of Mount Badon, Gildas continues, the Britons, those who had known both the invasion and the victory, for some time ' lived orderly ' in their several vocations—kings, magistrates, priests, other clerics, and all the commons in general.

By the time Gildas was writing, however, another generation—
some twenty or thirty years younger than he—had grown up.
They had not known the danger or the deliverance, and (as
younger generations are always said to do) they behaved less well.
' Laws ', said Gildas in the very voice of a man of almost fifty,
' are now shaken and turned upside down, and there is no virtue
anywhere.' He enlarged on this theme for the rest of his work,
giving—it must be admitted—a number of horrid particulars.

We have then in Gildas a picture of the over-running of Britain
by the Saxons until a rally under a leader of Roman descent
holds them off, and prepares for ' the siege of Mount Badon '
after which the Saxons are unable again to make head. The
troubles in the time of Gildas did not arise so much from them
as from civil wars between the patriots. The descendants of
Ambrosius Aurelianus, degenerate as Gildas held them to be,
were still capable of dealing with the pagans from beyond sea.
But there is in all this no word of Arthur.

That name occurs for the first time four centuries later, and
is still not that of a king. In the ninth century another monk,
called Nennius, wrote a similar history, but in more detail. He
gives the story of the calling in of the Saxons, under their leaders
Hengist and Horsa, by the British Vortigern ; of the marriage
of Vortigern to Rowena, Hengist's daughter ; of the new
arrivals of Saxons in force ; of the outbreak of war and of the
defeat of the Britons. He too speaks of a rally, but under a
leader Vortimer ; he mentions Ambrosius later, however, as
' king among all the kings of the Britons '. The war desperately
continues, until the rise of a new hero. Nennius goes on :

' Then Arthur fought with the Saxons, alongside the kings of the
Britons, but he himself was the leader in the battles. The first battle
was on the banks of the river which is called Gelin. The next four
were on the banks of another river, which is called Dubylas and is in
the region Linnius. The sixth was on a river which is called Bossa.
The seventh was in the wood of Celidon ; that is, Cat Coit Celidon.
The eighth was by Castle Guinnion, in which Arthur carried on his
shoulders an image of St. Mary Ever-Virgin, and on that day the

6

pagans were put to flight, and there was a great slaughter of them, through the strength of our Lord Jesus Christ and of the holy Mary His Maiden-Mother. The ninth was in the City of the Legion. The tenth was on the bank of the river which is called Tribiut. The eleventh was on the hill called Agned. The twelfth was on Mount Badon, in which—on that one day—there fell in one onslaught of Arthur's nine hundred and sixty men ; and none slew them but he alone, and in all the battles he remained victor.'

Another MS. adds that before Badon

' Arthur had gone to Jerusalem, where he had caused to be made a cross of the same size as the life-giving Cross, and after it had been consecrated he had fasted and kept vigil and prayed by it for three days together, asking that by this wood the Lord would give him victory over the pagans, which was so done. And he carried with him the image of St. Mary.'

Nennius has a few more things to say of Arthur. He records certain wonderful things of which he had heard or which he had seen in the Britain of his day ; that is, in South Wales. One is

' a marvel in the region which they call Buelt. For there is a heap of stones, and on the top of the heap one stone bearing the footprint of a dog. When they hunted the boar Troynt, Cabal which was the dog of Arthur the soldier, put his foot on that stone and marked it ; and Arthur afterwards piled up a heap of stones and that stone on top, on which was his dog's footprint, and called it Carn Cabal. And men will come and carry away that stone for a day and a night, and the next morning there it is back again on its heap.'

Another wonder is in the district called Erging.

' There is a burial mound near a spring which is known as Licat Anir, and the name of the man who is buried in the mound was called Anir. He was the son of the soldier Arthur, and Arthur himself killed him there and buried him. And when men come to measure the length of the mound, they find it sometimes six feet, sometimes nine, sometimes twelve, and sometimes fifteen. Whatever length you find it at one time, you will find it different at another, and I myself have proved this to be true.'

(The last statement is one of those mind-shattering things one finds in history. 'Et ego solus probavi.' Nennius has been careful enough all through to say that 'it is said' or 'which is called'. He says nothing about proving the tale of the stone. And then, as it were unnecessarily, he dares his reader to disbelieve him on this one point. Was the sentence added later ? Was he, suddenly and wildly, a liar ? Was there some simple, but obscure, explanation ? Or was there something very odd about that burial-ground ?)

Another document, a century later than Nennius, the *Annales Cambriae*, has two entries, in the second of which is an additional statement about Arthur. The entries are :

' 518 : The battle of Badon in which Arthur carried the cross of our Lord Jesus Christ, for three days and three nights, on his shoulders, and the Britons were the victors.

' 549 : The battle of Camlaun in which Arthur and Medraut were slain ; and there was death in England and Ireland.'

These are the early records or appearances of record. The fact that Gildas does not mention Arthur was attributed in the twelfth century to a personal—or rather a family—enmity. The brother of Gildas was said to have been killed by Arthur in a feud, and it was added that Gildas wrote as he did about the kings of Britain because of this killing, and that he had thrown into the sea ' those books in which he had written of the deeds of Arthur and his countrymen '. This is why there is in his work no authentic history of the king. But by this time the myth had begun to come seriously into being, and it was as necessary to explain the apparent omissions as to invent occasional allusions. It is certain that Gildas does not mention him ; we cannot certainly say whether this was because he was at feud with him, or because he did not know of him, or because there had never been any Arthur for him to know.

History, however, has of late inclined to let us believe in the reality of Arthur. The late R. G. Collingwood, in the first volume of the *Oxford History of England*, put forward a convincing suggestion. He argued that the evidence we have of his battles becomes clear as soon as we ' envisage Arthur as the commander of a mobile field-army'. At that period the Roman High Command was, in its European wars, using cavalry to a greater and greater extent. ' The late Empire was in fact the age which established the ascendancy of heavy cavalry, clothed in chain-mail, over infantry. Already in the first twenty years of the century the count of Britain commanded six regiments of cavalry to three of infantry, and anyone thereafter, reviving his office with some knowledge of what it implied, would know that a count of Britain should be a cavalry general.' Professor Collingwood went on to point out that, even without this special intention, a very small experience of contemporary warfare would expose the advantage of a mounted force. The local levies, defending particular towns, would have none. The highland tribes had none. The Saxon invaders certainly had none, just as they had no body-armour, and very little tactical cohesion. ' Any one who could enrol on his own initiative a band of mail-clad cavalry, using as mounts the ordinary horses of the lowland zone and relying for armament on the standard work of contemporary smiths, and could persuade the British kings of their value, might have done what Arthur is said to have done.' The list of battles in Nennius suggests that his mobile field-army moved, as it could do, all over the country, and was able to strike at different places. The final crashing victory at Mount Badon may mean that the Saxons had at last managed to confine this force to ' some British hill-fort, reconditioned, as Cissbury was, for defence against the invaders'. The phrases describing it— ' one onslaught of Arthur's ', ' none but he alone '—may suggest that in this last battle he was not supporting some local king, but operating solely with his own force.

The site of Badon cannot be fixed. It has been supposed to be on a line of British earthworks running from the Bristol Channel to the Marlborough Downs near Newbury. It has been identified with Bath, with Badbury Ring, with other Badburys, with Bedwyn, with Baydon, Beedon, Bowdon, and

Bown Hill. All is very doubtful ; on the whole, Liddington Hill, which has a Badbury near it, and might threaten a Saxon advance to the West, seems as good a guess as any and better than some.

We have then, to put all together, at least a possibility, behind the chronicles and the hypotheses—and perhaps rather more than a possibility—of an historic figure. The Saxon invaders, after a period of almost complete victory, had been checked by a chieftain, local but still notable among the British chiefs, of Romano-British descent. For some time after his success, the war hung level. There then came into prominence a man with a capacity for seeing and seizing military advantages. His name was Arthur ; he too may have been of Roman descent, since the name Arturus belongs to a Roman *gens*. He raised a force of mounted men, and went to the aid of the kings, when and how the military situation required. Eventually the Saxons were compelled to make an advance in strength into the west. The Captain-General took up a position on a fortified hill threatening this advance. The enemy besieged, or attempted to besiege, this hill. They were defeated, and wholly routed by a final cavalry charge led by Arthur himself. The result of the battle was that they retired to their own part of the country, and that for thirty or forty years the Britons were left in comparative peace, under the prestige of the Captain-General. During the earlier part of that time, the organizations of their State (or States) operated freely and effectively. But afterwards disputes and wars broke out among them, in one of which Arthur was killed. The cavalry, after this, either no longer existed or had no adequate leader. The Saxons renewed their attacks ; the divided and warring Britons could put up no sufficient defence ; and presently the invaders subdued and occupied the whole country except the extreme West. But the memory, and indeed the name, of Arthur still remained as a fable of the past and a prophecy of the future.

It was, however, by no means certain that that name would last, still less that it would enter into a great literature. It might have faded under the Saxons, let alone under the Normans. It was not to fade, and the time of decision was the twelfth century. Up to then Tennyson's later lines describe the situation not inaptly :

> that grey king whose name, a ghost,
> Streams like a cloud, man-shaped, from mountain peak,
> And cleaves to cairn and cromlech still.

Many names, so streaming, have not been re-imaged in poetry or even convincing prose. This name seems first to have been raised to royalty about 1075 (as far as our records go), in a *Legenda Sancti Goeznovii*, or rather in the historical prelude to the life of the saint. There the pride of the Saxons (' pagans and devilish men '—soon after the Norman Conquest) is crushed ' per magnum Arturum Britonum regem ', a precursor, as it were, of the Conqueror. Arthur proceeds to win other victories in Gaul as well as in Britain, after which, he having been ' ab humanis actibus evocato ', the Saxons return. The phrasing is of some interest ; the King is called away from human activity ; he is not absolutely said to have died. It was still about this time currently reported by some of the poor who knew and repeated the name that he was to return. There is a tale, of about 1146, recounting events of 1113, which shows this. The canons of Laon, wishing to rebuild their cathedral, sent some of their number to England to raise funds, taking with them certain relics of Our Lady of Laon. They came to Devonshire ; they heard of the tales of the Britons concerning ' the famous King Arthur '. At Bodmin a man with a withered arm came to be healed by the holy relics. He and one of the visitors—Haganellus, related to the lord Guy, archdeacon of Laon—fell into a dispute. The man with the withered arm maintained that Arthur still lived ; it seems likely, though we have no details, that the archdeacon's relative told him not to be such a fool. There was a demonstration in force by the man's friends ; they rushed into the church ' cum armis ', and there would have been bloodshed if a cleric named Algard had not somehow managed to interfere. It was clearly felt in Bodmin that foreigners had no business to sneer at local tradition. But the foreigners had the last victory. Our Lady of Laon was displeased ; and ' the man who had the withered arm, who had caused the tumult on behalf of Arthur, was not healed '.

The man made such trouble ' as the Britons make with the French about King Arthur ', the chronicle says. The Britons are, no doubt, the Bretons, and it follows that the tale was already widely known in that part of Europe. But it had—or certain names had—spread even more widely.

CHAPTER II

The Grail

THE point at which the myth of the Grail begins holds in its first appearance the most important account of all. No invention can come near it ; no fabulous imagination excel it. All the greatest mythical details are only there to hint at the thing which happens ; that which in the knowledge of Christendom is the unifying act, perilous and perpetual, universal and individual. That origin took place in the Jerusalem to which (it was reported) the Captain-General Arthur had gone before his final victory. Its record is in the Gospels ; it is taken here from the Revised Version of the Gospel of St. Mark.

' And as they were eating he [Jesus] took bread, and when he had blessed, he brake it, and gave it to them, and said, Take ye : this is my body, and he took a cup, and when he had given thanks, he gave it to them : and they all drank of it. And he said unto them, This is my blood of the covenant, which is shed for many. Verily I say unto you, I will no more drink of the fruit of the vine, until that day when I drink it new in the kingdom of God.'

This is the first mention of that Cup which in its progress through the imagination of Europe was to absorb into itself so many cauldrons of plenty and vessels of magic.

It was not for some centuries that the intellectual attention of Christendom directed itself to the nature of the Blessed Sacrament. Its first preoccupation was with the nature of God and of the Redeemer. Piety and spiritual devotion might centre on it, but the lesser powers of the Church (so to call them) were not yet free to turn to it. The identification in some sense of the Eucharist with our Lord was immediate ; the documents of the New Testament confirmed, when they came, the settled habit of the Church. It was regarded as a sacrifice—by Christ

and of Christ ; therefore, as a sacerdotal act. It was used, as
well it might be, as an argument against the Gnostic doctrines
of the unreality of matter and of the evil of the flesh. The sense
in which the dedicated elements were consecrated into something
other was not defined. Nor the moment of change ; our Lord
was supposed by some to condescend to the whole Rite and
general prayer of the Church ; by others, to the actual repetition
of the Words of Institution. But on these things there was as
yet no controversy.

Only the Act continued everywhere. The phrase of the New
Testament—' He was known of them in the breaking of bread '
—remained true and became more widely true, although the
knowledge was not intellectually epigrammatized. The relation
of the elements to the Sacred Body was called sometimes identity,
sometimes figure or symbol. But neither figure nor symbol
implied separation ; each word implied an interior closeness
which they have perhaps with us lost. The Act was priestly,
by Christ and for Christ ; the mysterious sacrifice was of Christ ;
and Christ in it was the food of man. The sacrifice was offered
not only on earth but in the heights of the heavens. He offered,
who was the offering, and there was as yet no controversy in the
Church.

But as the Nature of our Lord was defined, and as the Church
became more and more aware of what in fact she believed, so the
intellectual problems of that Act were more and more discussed.
It was stressed now one way and now another ; but no stress
necessarily denied another. It was a symbol, but it was He.
It was the offering of His passion, and communion with His
ascended life ; also it was communion with His passion and an
offering of His ascended life. This was His very death ; it was
also His very Resurrection ; it was, all ways, His Incarnation.
It was a double Act ; there was a kind of exchange in it. The
Church gave itself, and Christ gave Himself, and the two were
united. ' If you have received well ', said Augustine, ' you
are that which you have received.' Such a sentence, in some
sense, holds all ; it is this which, in the English words of

Malory, centuries later, was 'the secret of our Lord Jesus Christ'.

It was this communion which was referred to in the Lord's Prayer. St. Cyril of Jerusalem wrote : ' *Give us this day our substantial bread :* Common bread is not substantial, but this holy bread is substantial. . . . It is imparted to your whole system for the benefit of body and soul.' [1]   And as it was communicated for each body and soul, so it was all bodies and souls in the Church that were offered. 'The whole redeemed City itself is offered as a universal sacrifice to God by the High Priest', wrote St. Augustine. 'In a certain sense', he wrote again about the first Institution, 'He carried Himself in His hands.' This was the centre of the Christian and Catholic life : ' in this thing which the Church offers she herself is offered.'

So the great meditations ran on. There were—not so much disputes as faint disagreements, but there still seems to have been very little controversy. In East and West alike the sense of the Act grew keener ; the belief in the identification of the elements with Christ clearer. Miraculous visions began to appear —as in the tale in the *Paradise of the Fathers* (meaning the hermits of the Thebaid) in which an angel is seen slaying a child with a knife. The child or the man was seen ' smiting itself into the bread '. And with the visions, the controversies ; the young Church had known neither.

They did not however seriously begin in the West until about the eleventh century. No more need be said of them here than may suggest how the subject exercised the minds of men ; how therefore it preoccupied their minds. This is not to say that it was argued about in every place where men talked. But it was very likely to be at least spoken—if not argued—about in any place where the intellectuals talked. It was not, I suppose, dis-

[1] Quoted in *A History of the Doctrine of the Holy Eucharist*: Darwell Stone ; from which the other quotations are taken—C. W. [Beside this footnote Williams has pencilled 'Tolkien'. This means that Professor Tolkien here raised some philological questions about the meaning of ἐπιούσιον (Matt. vi. 11) and, probably that Williams intended to discuss the matter with him more fully on some later occasion—C. S. L.]

cussed as politics are to-day, but neither was its discussion confined to a particular class of the pious, as such things usually are
to-day. A more general imagination, a more universal (almost
—dare one say ?—a more *casual*) intellect was aware of it ; and
even the people who did not argue had probably heard of the
argument. For something like two centuries the nature of that
Act and of its consequences was, in various times and places,
disputed. Decisions were taken by Councils ; rites were
ordained by bishops ; devotions were multiplied by the pious.
So that, slowly perhaps but generally, among all the other
affairs of secular and religious life, the image of that Act, and of
the Host and the Chalice which were its means, grew primary in
the imagination of Europe.

A few points in that development may be mentioned. About
1040 Berengar of Tours, Archdeacon of Angers, was believed to
have taught that the Body in the Mystery was not to be identified
with that which was born of our Lady St. Mary, and to have
denied any ' conversion ' of the elements. He was opposed by,
among others, Lanfranc, afterwards Archbishop of Canterbury ;
who, in maintaining the reality of that conversion, declared that
the many occasions on which the body of Christ had been
miraculously seen in the Sacrament, proved the reality of the
presence. Durand, Abbot of Troarn, wrote that the Sacrament
was ' none other than that very flesh which the Virgin conceived
of the Holy Ghost, and brought forth with the integrity of her
spotless virginity unbroken, contrary indeed to the common
course of human nature, but not contrary to the reality of the
human body '. It is this sentence, and others like it, which
condition and characterize, as we shall see, the later image of
Galahad. The errors of Berengar were condemned at various
councils—in 1050 at Brienne (convoked by William of Normandy, afterwards William I of England, and patron of Lanfranc), in 1059 in Rome, in 1063 at Rouen, and in 1078 and 1079
again at Rome under the presidency of Gregory VII. At all of
these the doctrine of the identification was asserted, and ' the
union of flesh and soul in the resurrection of Christ '. The

phrase is ascribed to St. Peter Damian (1007–1072).[1] To him also is ascribed in the West the first use of the word *transubstantiation*.

A few other phrases from the end of the eleventh or beginning of the twelfth century may be quoted, to show the kind of doctrine and of image that was in the heart and the imagination of Christendom. Odo of Cambrai (1050–1113) wrote : ' It is divided and it cannot be consumed. It is eaten, but it remains uncorrupted. It is crushed and it is unimpaired. It is broken, and it is whole. This offering is flesh, but it is not carnal. It is unstained light rather, and pure. It is body, but not corporal. It is spiritual light rather, and pure. It is pure and cleansing, pure and purifying, pure because divine, more pure than material light.' And again : ' It is offered here, it is accepted there, not by change of place or succession of time, as if a movement of translation were begun in one place and completed in another. . . . There is no transference of place that bread may become flesh yet there is transference from the altar to heaven, because from being bread it is made God. . . . The Word of God is the altar on high.' Honorius of Autun (d. 1130) wrote : ' This is the same thing in the mouth of the worst of men as it is in the mouth of the most holy. . . . But, as the sun is the same in its heat and in its brightness, and yet produces different results in these two aspects, namely, burning the earth by its heat and giving light by its brightness, so the flesh of Christ remaining the same produces different results in different persons, incorporating the righteous with himself, separating the unrighteous from his life.' Robert Paululus (*c.* 1178) wrote : ' The golden altar [in the Jewish Tabernacle] signifies the altar of faith in the heart that is purged by penitence, and bright and clear with the testimony of a good conscience. On this altar the priest, now dead to the world but living to God, no longer the old Melchizedeck, flesh born of flesh, but the new man, spirit born of spirit, offers the invisible offering of flesh and blood through the oblation of earthly food.' Rupert of Deutz (d. 1135) wrote : ' Because the

[1] The MS. here gives a blank place enclosed in brackets.—C. S. L.

Virgin conceived him of the Holy Ghost, who is eternal fire, and he himself through the same Holy Ghost, as the Apostle says, offered himself a living sacrifice to the living God, by the same fire is the roasting (" roast with fire "—that is, burnt by the travail of the Passion) on the altar, for by the operation of the Holy Ghost the bread becomes the body and the wine the blood of Christ.' William of Champeaux (d. 1121) defined the ' doctrine of concomitance' in the phrase : ' He who receives either species receives the whole Christ. . . . In each species is the whole Christ, who after his resurrection is wholly invisible and impassible and indivisible, so that neither is the blood without the flesh, nor the flesh without the blood, nor either without the human soul, nor the whole human nature without the Word of God personally united to it.' Hildebert of Tours (1057–1134) defined the method of the Act : ' I utter the words of the Canon and the Word of the Transubstantiation.' And, as a final quotation, as if peculiarly applicable to that great myth which was soon to come into being, as if it were a warning and a watchword to the poets and makers of romances, Ivo of Chartres (1040–1116) declared in a sermon : ' It is a sacrament of faith ; search can be made into it healthfully, but not without danger '.

The climax of all this followed in the early years of the thirteenth century. Lothair Conti (1160–1216) became Pope under the title of Innocent III in 1198. Before his elevation to the Pontificate, he had written a book *On the Holy Mystery of the Altar*. He defines there ' the double sense of the four kinds of altars, whereby the " higher altars " denotes the Holy Trinity and the Church Triumphant, the " lower altar " the Church Militant and the " Table of the Temple ", the " inner altar " a clean heart and faith in the Incarnation, the " outward altar " the altar of the Cross and the Sacraments of the Church '. The offering is made not by the priest in his own person but in the person of the whole Church. ' The offering is primarily directed to God the Father as the first principle of the Godhead, yet the sacrifice of praise is offered equally to the Undivided Trinity.' The risen Body, thus communicated, has four qualities which were manifested in the Body before the resurrection : ' subtlety (when He was born of the Virgin), glory (when He was transfigured on the mount), agility (when He walked on the sea), impassibility (when He was eaten at the Supper).' ' By the power of this Sacrament it becomes possible that they who are of earth ascend to heaven.'

After his accession, Innocent prepared for what was one of the greatest Councils of the Middle Ages. It was held in the Lateran, in the year 1215. More than four hundred bishops, twice as many abbots and priors, many representatives of kings and princes were there. The Albigensian ' crusade ' had ended just before. It had been a dreadful and murderous business. But its cruelties must not prevent the recognition of the nature of the war, so far as it can now be discerned. It seems probable that there had grown up in Provence a kind of culture deriving from the old Gnostic dreams. Matter was either evil or negligible ; it was irrelevant to salvation and incapable of it. The adept would be—perhaps was already—free from it. It was directly against this doctrine that St. Dominic preached and Innocent sent the armies ; and against it, less directly and more universally, that the first chapter of the decrees ' On the Catholic Faith ' was proclaimed. It decreed :

' There is one universal Church of the faithful, outside which no one at all is in a state of salvation. In this Church Jesus Christ himself is both priest and sacrifice ; and his body and blood are really contained in the sacrament of the altar under the species of bread and wine, the bread being transubstantiated into the body and the wine into the blood by the power of God, so that, to effect the mystery of unity, we ourselves receive of that which is His, what He Himself received of that which is ours.'

By this decree the doctrine of the Eucharist was, as it were, raised to the level of the great formulating doctrines. It was, formally and theologically, received among those dogmas which defined the Triune Nature of the Omnipotence and the Double Nature of the Redeemer. But between those other doctrines and this, there was one extreme difference. All were ' of faith ', but in those others the faith was directed towards the Invisible and in this towards the visible. The Triune Omnipotence, the Two-Natured Redeemer, were real but (since His Ascension) removed. But the transubstantiating Body was visible in the transubstantiated matter of the elements—real and unremoved. There, visible but hidden, perfect under either species, were the subtlety, the glory, the agility, the impassibility. They were there for sacrifice and for communion. The true Priest (hidden in wafer and in wine) offered them, and generously permitted the Church and City a participation in His Act.

The theology was accompanied by the ordering of ritual. Decorum was enjoined on physical movement, as it was on intellectual development ; proper order was to rule in all. In the eleventh century at Canterbury Lanfranc had taken care of this, as he had earlier defended the Identity. He directed the method of the sacramental processions on Palm Sunday and the order of the genuflections. The abbot Simon of St. Albans followed him in the next century. It was to St. Albans that the King Henry II Plantagenet (whose name, one way or another, is so commingled with the Matter of Britain) sent a most costly cup to hold ' the case immediately containing the Body of Christ '. At Paris and at Cologne, at Salisbury and at Oxford, in Ireland and at Rome, from popes, bishops, and synods, decrees of order issued. The ringing of a bell at the consecration, and at the same time kneeling or prostration, intercessions and adorations, were placed and timed. The *Ancren Riwle* and the *Lay Folks' Mass Book* contain similar instuctions. In the first (dated in the early part of the thirteenth century) the anchoresses for whom it was meant are instructed, when they are dressed in the morning, ' to think upon God's flesh and on His blood, which is over the high altar, and fall on your knees towards it, with this salutation : " Hail, Author of our creation ! Hail, Price of our Redemption ! Hail, Support of our Pilgrimage ! Hail, Reward of our expectation ! " '

There was, in that century and after Lateran, one more grand development, which was hagiologically referred to the initiative

of Christ Himself. Such an initiative was indeed (it is a point
to be remembered, whether in the theology or in the myth) at
the root of the whole matter. It was our Lord who had first
acted and who continued to act. It is this which dominates the
fables and inventions : all of them are subject to and conditioned
by this. Galahad is conditioned by this. The whole Act is
Christ's and is imparted to those who are also His. But now, as
he had commenced the Act, and indoctrinated the theology, He
was said to have directed the ritual. A Belgian nun named
Juliana was a devotee of the Sacrament. Soon after Lateran,
she had a vision of a full moon, in which was one black spot.
She became aware that this appearance exhibited the lack in the
liturgical year of any feast in honour of the Sacred Body. Her
vision was communicated to the then Bishop of Liége, who in
1246 bade a feast of Corpus Christi be held in his diocese. In
1264 the Pope Urban IV, who had once been Archdeacon of
Liége, by the Bull *Transiturus* commanded it to be observed
through the whole of the Western Church. It could not be
fixed for the day of Institution, the Thursday of Holy Week,
because then the Church ' is not able to be fully at leisure for the
commemoration of this chief Sacrament '. ' Therefore, to confirm and exalt the Catholic Faith, we have worthily and reasonably determined to appoint that, concerning so great a Sacrament,
besides the daily memorial which the Church makes of it, there
be celebrated yearly a more solemn and special memorial,
appointing for this purpose a fixed day, namely, the Thursday
after the Octave of Pentecost. . . . We exhort and command . . .
that you keep so great and glorious a feast every year on the
aforesaid Thursday with devotion and solemnity.' For this new
feast, at the request and by the command of the Pope, St. Thomas
Aquinas composed the Office and the great hymn *Pange, lingua,
gloriosi*, and (though not for the Office) ' Devoutly I adore thee '.

Such then, in brief summary, was the development of Doctrine.
The Act had gathered into itself all circumstances. It had, as
it were, sunk into, and now dwelled among, all the most fundamental dogmas. It united all contraries in a mystery of exchange.

The Flesh and the Blood, invoked by the act of the celebrant, were there in their own full act—and were yet passive. They were carried, and were unmoving ; they were eaten, yet they themselves received the eater into themselves ; they were separate, yet they were one. They were the visibility of the invisible. They were the material centre of Christendom ; and they were the very Act that made them so.

The doctrinal intellect had so defined them. The general imagination, having helped that definition, now received it. But in the period, at least, before Lateran, the circumstances of the Act were received more generally than perhaps they afterwards came to be. Almost any article connected with the Act served for its symbol. Paten or cup, monstrance or tabernacle, were alike used. The word Grail itself is defined by the dictionaries as coming from the Latin *gradalis* and meaning a shallow dish ; thus, the paten ; and afterwards, erroneously, the cup. But the ' erroneously ' is hardly justified. The Grail may, etymologically, have been a dish. In the poems and romances it was ' chose espirituel '. Even in the Rites there were similarities between the objects used. ' In the Middle Ages there was not a clear distinction in form nor in part (from doctrinal motives) even in function between the vessel that contained the wine in the Eucharist, and the one that contained the holy wafer. The latter, as well as the former, had the shape of a cup, as it still has in the Catholic Church of to-day, and it was also not infrequently called the " chalice " (*calix*)—indeed, down into the eighteenth century.' [1] ' In the eleventh century, the host was broken on the paten, but in the twelfth century Durandus directs that it be broken over the chalice.' [2] The various actions of the Rite were to be accommodated, as far as might be, to the sense of the whole Christ. He was whole under each species— double but undivided, and the Rite was to exhibit him so.

Something perhaps should be said—and may be said here as

[1] J. D. Bruce : *The Evolution of Arthurian Romance.* 1928.
[2] Lizette A. Fisher : *The Mystic Vision in the Grail Legend and in the Divine Comedy.* 1917.

well as anywhere—about those fabulous vessels, which from Celtic or whatever sources, emerged into general knowledge. There has been much controversy about them—vessels of plenty and cauldrons of magic—and they have been supposed by learned experts to be the origin of the Grail myth. That, in the Scriptural and ecclesiastical sense, they certainly cannot be. Cup or dish or container of whatever kind, the Grail in its origin entered Europe with the Christian and Catholic Faith. It came from and with Christ, and it came with and from no one else. The Eucharist, in Europe, was earlier than any evidence of the fables ; that is a matter of history. But then it is a matter of history also that the Eucharist, as it came from and with the whole Christ, was meant for the whole man. It was for his eternal salvation, body and soul ; and the doctrinal development precisely stressed this. It was therefore, in the very idea of it, greater than any vessel of less intention could possibly be. If it swallowed up its lesser rivals, it did so exactly because it was greater. The poetic inventiveness of Europe found itself presented with the image of a vessel much more satisfying to it— merely as an image—than any other. There is no need to suppose the poets and romancers were particularly devout ; it is only necessary to suppose they were good poets and real romancers. A dogmatic anti-Christian opposition would, no doubt, have rejected the Grail image. But it is hard to see what else could. Cauldrons of magic—' dire chimaeras and enchanted isles '—are all very well at first, but maturing poetry desires something more. It desires something more actual to existence as we know it. But the Grail contained the very Act which was related to all that existence. Of course, it absorbed or excluded all else ; *sui generis*, it shone alone.

CHAPTER III

The Coming of the King

I

IN the twelfth century the shape of the new metaphysical civilization of Europe was becoming clear. Traffic had been eased ; the Universities established ; kingdoms and republic settled. Communication, physical and intellectual, was more convenient than it had been for centuries. Doctrines could be contrasted and corrected ; tales compared and continued. Men began again to know what other men at a distance had said and done, and were saying and doing. No doubt this had been[1] to an extent, perhaps to a great extent, during the earlier centuries. The Dark Ages were not so dark as to blot out all. But then their light was, at best, somewhat accidental and occasional ; now it can be prolonged and intentional. The courts begin to glow with colour ; dance, in every sense, has time to return.

Certainly that dance, of whatever kind, was permitted only within general intellectual limits, but at first the limits were fairly broad. The early Middle Ages are founded on metaphysics, but they are hardly as yet built up into metaphysics. That comes about only when the profession of belief—though not, of course, belief, for of that there can be no surety—was enforced by law and power. The old Roman Empire had been based on a similar profession of belief. The incense dropped on the altars before the images of the serene and salutary Emperor meant something. But it almost flagrantly did not mean precisely what it professed to mean. The incense swung before the new altars did. Few in the old Empire can ever have been seriously challenged on the exact way in which they believed

---

[1] I think Williams probably meant to write *been so,* but I am not certain and therefore preserve the MS. reading.—C. S. L.

the Emperor to be divine ; but any in the new order might be at least questioned about his beliefs on Christ's.[1] No doubt, in practice, the two things were not so unlike. It would not have done to be publicly blasphemous about the Emperor, and it is certain that there must have been a good deal of scepticism in the twelfth century. Men are not so made, as far as we have yet seen, that they can lose, over a continent and for centuries, the quality of disbelief. But the social tendencies were, on the whole, towards intellectual laxity and intellectual severity respectively. A conformity of thought and practice was desired and intended by a now highly organized institution. This intention was now carried and communicated by the new easing of traffic ; and more and more, as time went on, the absence of conformity was either corrected in the confessional or penalized by the laws. The old Empire had, on the whole and except for that one important point of loyalty, left a man to think for himself, and did not much feel it mattered what he thought. The new Church felt that it mattered a good deal what he thought and consequently did not wish to leave him to think for himself. In 1184—before this very century was out—the Pope Lucius III declared the criminal nature of heresy ; in 1215 Lateran defined the Faith ; in 1233 the Inquisition was established ; in 1252 the use of torture was permitted. In this horror the formalizing of the Middle Ages came into full being.

The earlier century had had a quality of its own. It was still ' rash with theories of the right That stretched but did not break its creed '. It was still free to use its imagination in ways which would afterwards be checked or darkened or even eluci-dated—for example, courtly love, witchcraft, and the Holy Eucharist. All of these had their effect on the Arthurian myth. But the most important thing for the myth in that century was that it was then first seriously shaped. Geoffrey of Monmouth was born, and wrote the *Historia Regum Britanniae*. ' No work of imagination,' says Sir Edmund Chambers, ' save the *Aeneid*,

---

[1] If the sentence had been revised the first half would have ended *in the Emperor's divinity.*—C. S. L.

has done more to shape the legend of a people than the *Historia Regum Britanniae.*'

Very little is known of Geoffrey, though at that something more than of his successor in the tradition who invented Galahad. This is as it should be ; the discoverer of the King of Britain can be praised as the discoverer of the High Prince cannot be. The date of his birth is not known, but it must have been well before 1129 when he was a witness to a charter. He took priest's orders in 1152, was made Bishop of St. Asaph, and died (it is said, at mass) in 1154. He wrote two books, and by general ascription one more. The first was the *Prophecies of Merlin* (   ) ; the second was the *Historia* ; the third was a *Vita Merlini* (   ).[1]

His own account is that he had begun the *Historia* when he was asked by his ecclesiastical patron, Alexander, Bishop of Lincoln, and by others, to furnish them with a translation of the British text of Merlin's prophecies. This he did and published it. He then returned to the *Historia*, into which he inserted as a complete chapter the earlier book. The question of Merlin may be, for the moment, postponed. The *Historia* begins with the fable of the coming of the Trojan Brutus to Britain, and ends with the conquest of the country by the Saxons, or rather (after that) with the fore-telling by an angel to the last of the British kings that the Britons shall again reconquer the land ' at the time of which Merlin prophesied to Arthur '.

It was, in fact, Geoffrey's own book which was the first Return, and new conquest, of Arthur. The name, and the names of some of his companions and lords, had been widely enough spread. But now the tale suddenly grew into more than a fable ; it became a fashion. He seems to have meant to create, among his other *historiae*, one splendid and popular figure, and he seems to have succeeded. It might have happened without him, but it did happen through him. He first—and if he were not the first, yet he was the first to do it for the courts, the authors, and the reciters of Western Europe—he first made Arthur a king.

---

[1] Two gaps between brackets in the MS. I have not been able to discover the dates. Not all agree that Geoffrey was the author of the *Vita.*—C. S. L.

He gave him magnificence and a court. The grey tales suddenly became a diagram of glory. The dim Captain-General of Britain was changed into a champion of splendour. It is in that shape that he now lives or dies.

The ' History ' begins with the successes of Aurelius Ambrosius and his brother Uther over the Saxons. Aurelius is rebuilding cities and churches, and especially London, ' a city that had not escaped the fury of the enemy ', when he is assassinated by a Saxon. Uther succeeds him. There appears in the sky a comet the tail of which is in the shape of a dragon, and from the dragon's mouth emerge two rays of light, one directed towards Gaul, the other towards Ireland. The dragon and one ray are interpreted by Merlin to mean Uther's son Arthur and his conquests ; the other to mean his daughter, Arthur's sister. Uther, in memory and premonition, causes two golden dragons to be made, one of which is set up in the cathedral church of Winchester and the other carried about with the army.

The first story of the birth of Arthur follows—one of the then popular stories of ' magic and mystery '. Uther held a great feast in London in order ' to put on his crown ' : publicly to manifest his royalty. He was attended by his lords, among whom is Gorlois, Duke of Cornwall, and his wife Igerna. The king immediately fell deeply in love with Igerna and so markedly exhibited his love before all the court that the infuriated Gorlois withdrew from the court to his duchy, where he shut up his wife in the castle of Tintagel and himself in Dimilion. There he was besieged by Uther. But love was too strong for the king to await the result of the siege ; he complained to his friend Ulfin of how near he was to death and on his counsel had recourse to Merlin. Merlin, ' by his arts and achievements ', creates one of those grand substitutions which are very old in myth but were, in the developing tale, to find presently a wholly new significance when Lancelot came to the little castle of [Case]¹ beyond Carbonek. The wizard's arts turn Uther, Ulfin, and himself into the physical

¹ The M.S. here leaves a blank space. I have supplied the name from Malory XI. ii.—C.S.L.

27

likeness of Gorlois and two of his companions. So changed, but so still themselves, they came in the evening to Tintagel, surrounded on all sides but one by sea, and on that having a mass of rock with but one narrow entrance. There, 'in the evening twilight', Uther, wearing the appearance of the Duke, was admitted. He protested to the Duchess Igerna that he had left his other castle only from love of her and only for a single night ; and she, believing and his wife, 'never thought to refuse him anything'. On that night 'the most renowned Arthur' is conceived. In the morning new messages from Dimilion arrived, this time real and true ; to bring news that Uther—or rather his army—had stormed the castle and that Gorlois was dead. They stood before the seeming Gorlois, bewildered and blushing with astonished shame. He, sitting by Igerna, declared that he would make peace with the king. He rode out, put off the magical likeness, became Uther again, stormed Tintagel, and eventually married Igerna. They lived 'in no small love', and besides Arthur had one other child, the princess Anne. Uther in the end dies while encamped at Verulam, through drinking from 'a spring of very clear water', which has been poisoned by the Saxons.

All this forms the eighth book of the *Historia*. The ninth is given up to Arthur. He was recognized as Uther's son by the lords, and crowned by Dubricius, Archbishop of the City of the Legions, Caerleon, at the age of fifteen. He was then 'a youth of such peculiar courage and generosity, of such a sweet temper and instructive [1] goodness, that he is greatly loved by all the people'. He was, in fact, at an earlier age, much like Shakespeare's Henry V, and his subsequent actions are not at all dissimilar. The Saxons were still in control of half the country, and Arthur determined to make war on them, because (i) he wished to enrich his own followers with their wealth, (ii) that wealth, and the whole country, was his by right. The two are

[1] Thus the MS. The Latin is *innata bonitas*. That Williams wrote or meant to write 'instinctive' seems probable ; but not so certain as to justify emendation.—C. S. L.

not to be separated, and one might add a third, which is merely self-defence, since the Saxons are set on exterminating the whole British race. There is no need to go into details of the campaigns, in which Geoffrey's own military invention describes some, but not all, of the battles given in Nennius. Duglas is there, and the Wood of Celidon, and Badon ; others are at York, Lincoln, and Thanet, besides three in North Britain, and one by Loch Lomond against the Saxons' Irish allies.

Britain thus liberated, the king proceeded to reduce Ireland and Iceland. The kings of Gothland and of the Orkneys submitted. Here the first period of conquest ceased, and the king reigned in peace for twelve years. His court became the centre of glory and fashion—fashion in every sense of the word. Geoffrey relates that not only did King Arthur introduce such high courtesy as was imitated in the manners of the most distant lands, but that no lord in the world thought himself of any worth unless his arms and clothes were made in the same style as those of the lords of King Arthur. Those lords are not, on the whole, those whom we later know, but three names are familiar. There is Lot, who is then the nephew of the king of Norway, and 'consul of Londonesia', a mature man, wise and valiant, to whom by Uther's choice Arthur's sister Anne had been married. He had two children by her, Wolgan and Modred. The other two lords who survived in later romances were Caius the king's steward, and Bedver his brother—afterwards Kay and Bedivere.

During this period of peace the king married. His wife was Guenhumara, descended from a noble Roman family, and (inevitably and properly) the most beautiful woman in Britain. But the peace did not last. All the kings of Europe became terrified of Arthur, however their lords might copy his in dress and manners. They began to make preparation against what our simpler age would call his 'aggressiveness'. Geoffrey, however, seems entirely to approve his hero, whom he causes to be full of delight at this fear, and to develop a design to conquer Europe. One cannot wholly separate this design from its final outcome in Arthur's death, but neither can one attach any serious moral value to it. Geoffrey is not writing in those terms. Arthur, according to him, began by conquering Norway, to which his brother-in-law had a kind of claim by the dead king's nomination. When Norway and Dacia had been reduced, Arthur proceeded to Gaul. This was a more serious matter, for Gaul was under the government of Flollo, a Roman tribune, who held it from the Emperor Leo, as the city of Rome itself is held in the same way by the procurator Lucius Tiberius. The seat of the imperial power in Byzantium is not mentioned ; the king is to be concerned with the west. By Geoffrey's day, of course, the Empire was divided, and yet still theoretically one. But it was as if he had enough historic sense to remember that in his Arthur's own supposedly historic day, it was not so. The king is not allowed to make war on the Emperor himself.

The tale relates how Arthur killed Flollo in single combat, occupied Gaul, and returned to Britain. There he held at Pentecost in the City of Legions a great solemnity. It is the climax and spectacle of his civil glory, though there are to be other military achievements. Caerleon was a noble city ; kings from all parts of the world came sailing to it up the Severn. In it were two marvellous churches—St. Julius, to which a nunnery was attached which served it with a choir of virgins, and St. Aaron, to which belonged a convent of canons. The city was also renowned for a college of two hundred philosophers, learned in all the arts, who astrologically divined the future and made predictions to the king. The Archbishop of the City of Legions, Dubricius, was Primate of England and Legate of the Apostolic See ; he was so holy that he could heal any sick person by his prayers. In this half-miraculous glory, the king, in the presence of all subordinate kings, consuls, and lords this side of Spain, was solemnly crowned and robed, in the metropolitan church of St. Aaron ; the queen meanwhile being endued with similar state in St. Julius, the church of the Virgins. Afterwards the two royalties held their separate festivals in separate halls, as had been the custom in Troy, from which even more ancient and glorious city the Britons and Arthur, King of Britain, derive.

Caius, with a thousand young men in ermine, served the king's meat ; Bedver, with a similar number, his wine. The queen was similarly served. It is all a very high glory. The men are all celebrated for their valour, the women for their wit. Love encourages all to virtue, the women especially to chastity, the men especially to valour. But nobility in all things thrives in them all. The court of the great king is the centre and cynosure of the world.

What remains ? One other thing, and then the end. There come to the feast of Caerleon twelve ambassadors, wise old men, to demand from Arthur his submission to Rome. In the council that follows the king and his lords prepare to match themselves with Rome. Troy has been named, and in the scene that old war seems again to take on a new being—the descendants of Brutus against the descendants of Aeneas. Hoel, king of Armorien, declares that the Sibylline prophecies foretold that the Roman Empire should be held by three natives of Britain ; Brennus and Constantine are past, and now it is the turn of Arthur to hold the supreme dignity. Fate strengthens him. He appoints the queen and his nephew Modred to be his regents and prepares for war.

His opponent, Lucius Tiberius, procurator of Rome, gathers his own supporters. At a later moment he thinks of waiting for the aid of the Emperor Leo, but decides against it. But short of the imperial armies, the roll of Eastern kings reads like the list of the allies of Antony recorded in Virgil and in Shakespeare. Here are the kings of the Grecians and the Africans ; of Spain and Libya ; of Phrygia and Egypt, Babylon and Bithynia, Syria, Boeotia, and Crete ; of the Parthians and Medes. The invasion begins, and after Arthur has shown his personal valour by killing a giant at St. Michael's Mount, the armies engage under the golden dragon of Britain and the golden eagle of Rome. Many lords fall, including Caius and Bedver and Lucius Tiberius himself, whose body the victorious Arthur sends to the Senate with a message that this is the only tribute the Britons pay. He is about to cross the Alps for the final advance on Rome when news comes from Britain. The regents have violated their oaths. Modred has seized the crown, and the Queen Guenhumara has married him. Arthur returns, defeats Modred at the head of a mixed army of Britons, Saxons, Scots, Picts, Irish, and all malcontents, pursues him to Winchester, and there defeats him again. The queen, repenting, flees to Caerleon, and takes the vows among the nuns of St. Julius. Modred falls back into Cornwall and is there killed in the final battle. Arthur is mortally wounded, 'and being carried away to the isle of Avalon to be healed of his wounds, he gave up the crown of Britain to his kinsman Constantine, the son of Cador Duke of Cornwall, in the year of the Incarnation of our Lord five hundred and forty two'.

The Captain-General of the British kings, the leader of that cavalry force against the Saxons, had thus become quite another thing. He had been mythically raised into a grander throne than any of those old tribal chieftains, half his clients and half his patrons, had ever held. No doubt many elements had gone to the raising—all that Geoffrey had heard or read, all he knew of courts and cloisters, many fables and many facts. But unless there was once some intermediary tale which is now wholly lost (such as that book of the Archdeacon Walter Map to which he continually appeals, but in which no scholar now believes),[1] the new definition of Arthur was his alone. It was he, as things turned out, who determined what Arthur should be, and also what he should not be. He was to be a king and all but an emperor, but not a lover ; a commander, not a knight-errant ; central, not eccentric. His court and Table (but the Table has not yet come into being) were to accumulate to themselves all kinds of adventures, and finally the most terrible adventure of all, but there was then and has remained a curious respectability about it. It was (if you choose) a wish-fulfilment ; it was, as Geoffrey frankly stated, the kind of court over which every king wanted to preside and to which every lord wanted to belong.

[1] At this point I interrupted the reading to suggest that the view taken by A. Griscom (*The Historia Regum Britanniae of Geoffrey of Monmouth*, London, 1929) was different. The single word 'Griscom' pencilled on the MS. doubtless means that Williams intended to give the matter further consideration.

He was the world's wonder, and it was proper that he should be, for he was entirely the kind of thing at which the world wanted to wonder—not perhaps in the five hundred and forty-second year of the Incarnation of our Lord, but certainly in the eleven hundred and thirty-ninth or thereabouts. The *Historia Regum*, as one might say, ' caught on '. Geoffrey had taken up a fable and so shaped and told it that it now had the potentiality of myth. Other and greater writers were to change it again into something more tremendous. But none of them should have written without, in the end, saying to their books, as the lord Galahad said to Bors of Lancelot : ' Salute me to my lord Geoffrey our father.'

And even the new figure of Arthur was not all. He gave us more—the name and supernatural strangeness of Merlin. It is true that in his account Merlin's chief activities are before Arthur's birth, and that he disappears from the tale at the point of the birth. He is there in relation to the king only to cause the magical substitution of Uther for Gorlois, and many other ways could have been found for the birth without that. But Geoffrey already had Merlin on his hands.

It seems likely that he invented him, as a person. Nennius had included a tale of a supernatural boy who had prophesied to Vortigern, the traitor British king who had called the Saxons over. Geoffrey took over and adapted this story. The name of Merlin may have come from the Celtic Myrddin. But Nennius knows nothing of Myrddin. He records that roughly at the time of Arthur, there were ' Talhiarn Cataguen and Neirin and Taliessin and Bluchbard and Cian, all famous at the same time in British poetry '. Myrddin was a bard, but not a prophet, let alone a wizard, in the Welsh tales. There is a poem called the *Dialogue of Myrddin and Taliessin*, a lament over a battle between two Northern chieftains, which ends

> Since I, Myrddin am next after Taliessin,
> Let my prediction become common.

' This is ... the only thing in works not demonstrably

dependent on Geoffrey that suggests the possession of prophetic powers on the part of Merlin in all Welsh literature.'[1]

The supernatural boy of Nennius and the bard of Welsh poetry were now united by Geoffrey, who provided his combined figure with a birth of a new kind ; new, that is, as far as the story went, but not unrelated to other fables of the time.   Vortigern was in danger from both Saxons and Britons and determined to build himself a new castle, but the earth always swallowed up the foundations. His wise men advised him that he must discover 'a lad who never had a father', and sprinkle his blood over mortar and stones before they would be firm.   Outside Carmarthen the king's messengers heard a boy taunted by his companions with having had no father. They seized on the boy and his mother, who is found to be 'a daughter of the king of Demetio', who lived in Carmarthen among the nuns of St. Peter. In Vortigern's presence the princess told her tale. She said : 'Lord, it is true I do not know who his father was. Once, when I and my companions were in our rooms, there appeared to me the shape of a handsome young man, who embraced and kissed me, and when he had been with me a little while, he suddenly vanished, and I never saw him again. But I often heard him speaking to me when I was alone, though I could never catch sight of him, and after he had haunted me in this way for a good time, I conceived and gave birth to this child. This, lord, is indeed what happened. No other could possibly be his father.' Vortigern again consulted one of his wise men who told him that other men had been conceived in this way. 'For,' he said, 'as Apuleius reports, in speaking of the god of Socrates, there are spirits between the earth and the moon whom we call daemons. Their nature is both angelic and human, and they are able whenever they choose to take on the shapes of men and have intercourse with women.'

In the later Middle Ages Geoffrey of Monmouth would not have been able to write so ; even in the next century it would have been dangerous. 'Those who dwell between the earth

[1] J. D. Bruce : *Evolution of Arthurian Romance.*

34

and the moon' would have been too like ' those who come in the air' at the trial of St. Joan of Arc : diabolic and dangerous to souls. But here they are not so. The thing changed, but at present there was a certain casualness even as regarded witchcraft and magic. It was, in general, believed to happen sometimes, and then it was thought to be a peculiar and rather horrid religious perversion. But it was also thought (very sensibly) that belief in it was almost as dangerous as the thing itself. And then there were, as one might say, a kind of select class of refined sorcerers attached to the households of great lords, together with alchemists, astrologers, clairvoyants, and so on, who were not unlike the college of two hundred philosophers in the City of Legions, the foundation of which might be suspected to have something to do with Merlin. Even as late as 1280 the Abbot of Whalley employed a clairvoyant to discover the body of his drowned brother ; it is true that, when this was discovered, he was excommunicated, but there the fact is. Merlin was something much greater than any such paid adept. He came from those other beings, faerie rather than diabolic, strange and comely, capable of high knowledge and sensuous delight.

It may perhaps be most convenient to pursue the subject of the birth and life of Merlin here. Geoffrey of Monmouth wrote a *Vita Merlini*, but in that the young wizard of the *Historia* has changed into a king and prophet of great age, the kind of figure with which the name of Merlin is more usually nowadays associated. He had not been so in the time of King Arthur, but this is long after the time of King Arthur. The king has been carried away in a boat by Taliessin who takes him ' to the island of apples which is called Fortunate' (' Insula pomorum quae Fortunata vocatur '). Taliessin afterwards joins Merlin, and ' takes occasion to consider the various nature of the creation '. The poem becomes largely a dialogue *de natura rerum* by the two masters, interspersed with certain non-Arthurian adventures of Merlin.

But the next great development in the myth of Merlin came with Robert de Borron. It was perhaps here particularly affected by the general imagination of the time. Christendom, among its other formalizations of ideas, was formalizing the devil; that is, it was giving more and more attention to the devil. Neutral supernatural beings, ' between the cold moon and the earth ', half human, half angelic, were disappearing in favour of the wholly angelic, evil or good. It was impossible that a good angel should wish to have intercourse with women; the text in Genesis about the sons of God seeing the daughters of men showed that. Any spirit who attempted it was bound to be evil. The next step was to say that evil spirits had attempted it. If so, they had failed. It was afterwards laid down by the authors of the *Malleus Maleficarum* that the devil cannot procreate by means of a woman, for he cannot produce human seed. But these refinements were not known to de Borron, or if so, he ignored them for the sake of his poem. He imagined a council held in hell after the Redemption, where, sitting ' in their own dimensions, like themselves ', the devils plotted to thwart it. They determined that the only method is to follow our Lord's method. There must be an incarnation; flesh must be made amenable to their desires; a pure maiden must conceive and bear a son. There, as so often, the conspirators of malice can only follow the conspiracy of divine largesse; a true priest is necessary even for the Black Mass; a clean maid is necessary even for the incarnation of the devil. One of the demonic powers agreed to make the attempt. He finds a girl who had made but a single slip; once she forgot or neglected to say her prayers. The lightness (so to call it) of the fault marks her real spirituality; grosser natures would not have served. Through that frailty he was enabled to approach her; she miraculously conceived. When she knew it she went at once to a wise and holy man. By his interposition and the rites of the Church there was born at the proper time not Diabolus but Merlin. He inherited his spiritual father's knowledge and power, but without malice. It is this figure to which, as we shall see, de Borron attributes the union of the tale of the king with the tale of the Holy Grail.

It was this Merlin who later survived, though in modern times his connexion with the Grail has been lost. He has, in fact, been remembered only for two things : (i) for his wizardry, (ii) for his end. There was indeed an Elizabethan play, once attributed to William Shakespeare and William Rowley, and now only to Rowley, which is called *The Birth of Merlin*. It is a poor thing, with a good deal of the usual Elizabethan humour about the child's unknown father. His mother Joan is a peasant girl with no sign of spirituality about her ; and neither she nor anyone else talks the sure Shakespearean style. (Shakespeare himself alluded to Merlin twice : Hotspur is made to speak of him in reference to Glendower :

> I cannot choose ; sometimes he angers me
> With telling of the moldwarp and the ant,
> The dreamer Merlin and his prophecies.

And at the end of one of the heath scenes in *King Lear* the Fool, after seven couplets, concludes : ' This prophecy Merlin shall make ; for I live before his time.' Which, if we substituted some other name, is exactly such a prediction as Merlin himself might have made.)

Indeed the only English poets who have spoken almost worthily of that great master are Tennyson and Swinburne, and of the two Swinburne is for once the greater. It is he who carries on the strange birth, and he who even improved on the conclusion. Of the birth he says that Tristram, talking to Iseult on the deck of the ship bringing her to Cornwall, spoke of the king and the court, and of

> the might of Merlin's ancient mouth,
> The son of no man's loins, begot by doom
> In speechless sleep out of a spotless womb ;
> For sleeping among graves where none had rest
> And ominous houses of dead bones unblest
> Among the grey grass rough as old rent hair
> And wicked herbage whitening like despair
> And blown upon with blasts of dolorous breath
> From gaunt rare gaps and hollow doors of death,

A maid unspotted, senseless of the spell,
Felt not about her breathe some thing of hell
Whose child and hers was Merlin ; and to him
Great light from God gave sight of all things dim
And wisdom of all wondrous things, to say
What root should bear what fruit of night or day,
And sovereign speech and counsel higher than man ;
Wherefore his youth like age was wise and wan,
And his age sorrowful and fain to sleep ; . . .

His conclusion may be left for the present. In the old French romances the end of the grand adept was unworthy of him. I do not say that this was not deliberate ; I think it easily may have been, and meant to reduce the possessor of such supernatural wisdom to natural folly in the end. It is a tale told of all the great—of Solomon and Aristotle and Virgil—and whoever took it over for Merlin need not be supposed to be ignorant of what he was doing. The danger of an over-devotion to the study of sources is that we forget to attribute to those who used them a conscious intention in using them. Merlin is very old, and comes to dote on a girl named Viviane or Niniane. She was at first only twelve years of age ; as the centuries went by, she grew older and lost her character, till we are left with the greedy and shallow harlot of Tennyson. He tells her a spell which can hold even him enchanted and imprisoned. And one day, in that mysterious forest—Darnantes or Broceliande—she casts him into sleep and puts the spell in motion. He has had his reward from her—or perhaps he has not, for in some versions he only dreams that he has had her, and it is illusion, but he lies content. There is a gracious version in a fifteenth-century English prose version of de Borron ; which, after describing the enchantment, continues :

' And after that she went and sat down by him and laid his head in her lap and held him there till he did awake ; and then he looked round him, and him seemed he was in the fairest tower of the world, and the most strong, and found him laid in the fairest place that ever he lay before. And then he said to the damsel : " Lady, thou hast me deceived, but if ye will abide with me, for none but ye may undo this enchantment"; and she said: "Fair sweet friend, I shall often times go out and ye shall have me in your arms, and I you; and from thenceforth ye shall do all your pleasure." And she held him well covenant, for few hours there were of the night nor of the day, but she was with him. Nor ever after came Merlin out of that fortress that she had him in set; but she went in and out when she would.'

II

GEOFFREY had written, in a general way, as if he were writing history; that is, he had presented his book in the shape of an arranged and continuous record of past times. It was not the yearly annals of the chroniclers on the one hand, nor did it pretend to be romance on the other. His two most famous successors in the tale allowed themselves more freedom. One was[1] an Anglo-Norman clerk, born in Jersey, named Wace, who lived from about 1100 to about 1175, and about 1155 'published' his *Geste de Bretons* or (as others more usually called it) *Roman de Brut*. The prestige of the fabulous Trojan Brutus was still very strong; the Britons were still derived from a city more ancient than Rome or Byzantium. Arthur, in his blood, drew from a deeper fount than any imperial house could; one might even imagine that the final fall of his glory was not entirely without a dim relation to that other overthrow of Troy. Fifty or sixty years after his *Brut*, an English priest in Worcestershire produced another, which he frankly professed to found on Wace. Both were in verse; the 15,000 lines of Wace become 30,000 in Layamon. But the style of the two poets was very different. Wace carried on the culture and medieval splendour of Geoffrey. Layamon wrote under the poetic influence of older poets, of the Anglo-Saxons. Wace is busy with courts and progresses; Layamon with heroes and fighting. There is in Layamon something not unlike dialogue and exclamations; where Wace gives silk and the polish of steel, Layamon gives cloth and the weight of steel. It is, however, not with their style but with their story that we are concerned.

[1] MS *They were.*

They both follow Geoffrey, but with added detail, the most important addition being the invention of the Round Table itself. The birth of Arthur is told by both in the same manner as in Geoffrey; though in Layamon Merlin is introduced to Uther by means of a hermit. The hermit lived away to the west, in a wilderness, in a deep forest; he had dwelled there many winters, and Merlin often came to him there. The hermit, coming back from Uther, saw Merlin standing under a tree and ran to him; when they had embraced, Merlin (so wise as he was) spoke of the hermit's errand and forestalled him in revealing Uther's desire. He went on to prophesy of Arthur: 'All shall bow to him that dwells in Britain; gleemen shall sing of him well; noble poets shall eat of his breast; men shall be drunk on his blood. . . . This word is secret; neither Ygearne or Uther knows yet that such a son shall come from Uther Pendragon; he is yet unbegot that shall govern all the people.'

Both the hermit and the forest are among the first—if they are not the very first—appearances in English, certainly in this myth, of those two images. Both, in various measure and in varied shapes, and under changing names, were to haunt the myth. The birth of Arthur was presently, by a dextrous twist, to be made canonical, or almost so, as near so as could be without involving Ygearne in a love too much like Guinevere's or Iseult's. Merlin was to know of even holier beings than hermits. And this western forest was to expand on all sides until presently it seemed as if Camelot and Caerleon and even Carbonek were but temporary clearings within it. But in Layamon Merlin goes on to Uther; the transformations are accomplished and the child born. In Layamon also, and first, the elves take charge of him. 'They enchanted the babe with strong magic; they gave him might to be the best of knights; they gave him a second boon, to be a rich king; they gave him a third, to live long; they gave him good virtue, so that he was the most generous of living men. These things the elves gave; well throve the child.' This again is one of the earliest relations of the king's person to faerie. He never came quite to belong to it; he was always to be of this world, and it was fortunate, for that most serious of all quests in which his companionship, if not he, were to be involved, is not at all of faerie kind. Yet faerie hovered for centuries behind his shoulder, or indeed in his scabbard. Morgan le Fay was his sister, less explicable than that other sister who began as Anne and ended as Morgause, but was always the wife of King Lot and the mother of Mordred and Gawaine and the rest of the princes of the house of Orkney. At Badon, in both Wace and Layamon, the king wore a sword forged in Avalon, almost a faerie place—forged ' with magic craft ', says Layamon, who calls it Caliburen, but Wace names it Excalibur. Layamon adds that his helmet was called Goswhit, and his shield Pridwen, on which was engraved in tracings of reddish gold, the image of the blessed and glorious Mary. Both poets add that the name of his spear was Ron.

It is Layamon who tells us of his cry when he is called to the throne by the bishops and lords : ' Lord Christ, God's Son, be to us now in aid that I may in life hold God's laws.' Both praise him with different phrases at this moment. Wace says that he was fifteen, tall and strong for his years, worthy of praise and glory ; haughty to the haughty, mild to the mild. He was one of Love's lovers ; he was above all other princes in courtesy and prowess, valour and largesse. Layamon adds that he was ' a father to the young, a comforter to the old, a judge to the foolish. He had no cook that was not a good champion, nor knight's servant that he was not good thane. The king held all his folk together with great bliss.'

There belonged, it may be held, to that bliss the most important new invention which these poets supplied—the making of the Round Table itself. The image may have come, and probably did come, from more ancient sources. Wace mentions its making, but only briefly : ' it was ordained that when this fair fellowship sat to meat, their chairs should be alike high, their service equal, none before or behind his companions ; and none could brag that he was exalted above any, for all alike were gathered round the board, and none was alien at the breaking of

Arthur's bread.' Layamon, however, gives a whole story. Arthur held Christmas court in London, during which jealousy and envy broke out in the household ; there were high words, blows, and eventually a great and bloody tumult, which the king himself in arms suppressed. He who began it was condemned to be thrown into a marsh ; his male kindred to be beheaded ; his nearest women folk to have their noses cut off. Anyone who in future causes a similar brawl is to be torn by wild horses ; so stern a judge to the foolish was the king. All the court swear on holy relics against any further outbreak. After this a man of Cornwall proposed that he should make for the king a great table, at which sixteen hundred men and more might be seated, within and without : ' there shall the high be equal with the low '. The king assented. The Table took four weeks to make, and when on the next day the court was assembled, ' all they one by one were seated, the high and the low '. ' It is not all sooth nor all falsehood that minstrels sing, but this is sooth of Arthur the king.'

Arthur's marriage takes place in both poems, though in Wace the queen is called Guinevere, in Layamon Wenhaver. In both she comes of Roman blood. Wace has the more princely description ; she is ' fair in face, courteous, delicate in person and motion, of a royal bearing, very sweet and of a ready tongue '. Arthur is said, in general, to love her wondrous well, but the single phrase has to serve. Even Wace, with his Love's lover, does not care to develop the theme, except that both he and Layamon follow Geoffrey in declaring that love encouraged chivalry and chastity. No knight could offer love to any lady till he had proved his worth ; then he might, ' and his friend was the more chaste as he was brave'. The phrase suggests —as we might from other sources suppose, and those not only Christian or doctrinal but imaginative and poetic—that chastity was more than a negation of lust ; it was a growing, heightening, and expanding thing. It was a state of spiritual being, and its spiritual expression was not at all inconsistent with marriage. It is to be remembered that chastity might be either married or virginal. Certainly the officials of the Church tended to stress the more austere type, but certainly also from the beginning there was a wider validity in the whole. But that lies more closely in Galahad and his companions on the quest.

It is against chastity and loyalty that the queen and Mordred offend. In both poems the queen's passion for Mordred is named. It is put forward as a fact and must be taken as a fact, for there has been no preparation. ' She had set her love,' says Wace, ' on her husband's sister's son.' ' The queen came to Mordred,' says Layamon, ' who was to her dearest of men.' Her end is alike in both : at York she hears of Mordred's defeat at Winchester ; she is highly troubled and full of remorse. ' Better were the dead than those who lived, in the eyes of Arthur's queen.' ' Woe was to her awhile that she was alive ! ' She escaped at night, accompanied by two lords, to the convent at Caerleon, where she had once been crowned. There she took the veil. ' Never again was fair lady heard or seen, never again found or known of men.' ' Nor for many years after did any man know if she were dead or if she were sunk in the water.'

As for the king, he was terribly wounded in the last battle, and had himself carried to Avalon to be healed of his wound. In both poems he commits the kingdom to the charge of Constantine, son of Cador Earl of Cornwall, to keep until he should come again. Layamon causes him to add that he will go to ' Argante the queen, fairest of maidens, an elf most fair ', who will make him whole with healing draughts. Wace gives the date—it was the year 642 of the Incarnation. Both say that Merlin prophesied the return. Wace holds that his words were doubtful, and that men have always doubted. ' Earl Constantine took the land into his charge and held it as he was bidden ; nevertheless, Arthur came not again.' But Layamon ended the tale on a higher note.

' Then was fulfilled what Merlin said once—that there should be much care of Arthur's departing. The Britons believe that he is alive, and dwells in Avalon with the fairest of all elves, and ever they expect when Arthur shall return. Never was any man born, of any lady chosen ever, who knew so much more of truth, to say more of Arthur. But of old while there was a wise man called Merlin ; he said with words—and sooth were the things he said—that an Arthur should yet come to help the English.'

CHAPTER IV

The Coming of Love

THE king had been established in his splendour. There was now another court, besides those of Alexander and Charlemagne, in which magnificence could exist, from which heroes could ride upon adventures, and to which their achievements could be returned. It was not yet certain that that potentiality would be accepted. The decision lay in the minds of poets and romancers, contemporary and future. The work of Geoffrey of Monmouth might have remained single and remote, and the work of Wace and Layamon might not seriously have complicated, though it might have heightened, the myth. The glory of the king would have remained a glory of wealth and war. That more than this happened was due primarily to the genius of two writers, Chrétien de Troyes and Robert de Borron. It was their choice of—say, their allegiance to—the king which determined the future.

They belonged, both of them, to that Anglo-French civilization which now ruled in the West. The name of one of its own princes is indirectly connected with Arthur—the name of Henry II Plantagenet, King of England and Duke of Normandy, Anjou, and (by his wife Eleanor) of Acquitaine. It was in his reign that the Abbot of the Benedictine monastery at Glastonbury, Henry of Blois, determined to have excavations made. Glastonbury had been identified with Avalon ; also, it was the place where Joseph of Arimathea had set the Grail. Discovery was said to confirm at least the first myth, the myth of royalty. At a depth of sixteen feet, a coffin of oak was found, on which was an inscription : ' Hic jacet sepultus inclitus rex Arthurus in insula Avalonis.' Within it were bones and (it is said) golden hair which when a monk lifted it fell into nothing.

In France there was a development in letters, also indirectly relating the Pendragon to the Plantagenet. The earliest name is that of a certain Marie de France who is generally identified with Marie, Countess of Champagne. It is to be hoped that the identification may be correct, for Marie would then indeed be not only a daughter of France, since the Countess of Champagne was the daughter of Louis VII, but step-sister-in-law to England, through Eleanor the wife of the Plantagenet. Marie de France wrote certain *lais* which she dedicated to King Henry, in one of which, though only in one, the court of Arthur is invoked. Lanval, in the *lai* of that name, is one of his knights, and is loved by his queen. From the beginning of the Matter of Britain, the queen seems to have been, as it were, doomed to infidelity. Her husband was not to love, in that kind, at all, and she was to love too much. In a literary sense, indeed, the later Lancelot was to be her salvation, for it was he by whom she was to endure a great passion and to come to some penitence, whereas otherwise she might have remained linked with a score of unknown names. It may be that she was taught to love so because those who wrote of her would not have the queen of Arthur less than Iseult the queen of Mark, whose passion for Tristan was already a theme of song. But in *Lanval* she loves without return, for the knight himself has a fairy mistress who carries him off—where but to Avalon, which is her own land and 'a very fair island'?

But if Marie of France was also Marie of Champagne, she had a client who did more for King Arthur than she. The Countess held her court at Troyes and made it a centre of this new and metaphysical civilization, and even more a centre of one of the lesser cults which were thriving in it. There was a kind of cult of sorcery, but this the Countess does not seem to have encouraged, any more than (for all that one can see) she encouraged that other cult of sanctity. What she did encourage was the art of poetry and the cult of courtly love. Among the poets who surrounded her was a certain Chrétien, called from his place of lodging de Troyes. He was there from 1160 to 1172; he is said to have been a herald and to have visited England—

both of which are pleasant notions and quite credible. But we do not know. By 1160 the *Historia* of Geoffrey of Monmouth had been 'out' some twenty years. Chrétien (as he himself tells us) had translated Ovid and written a poem on Tristan; neither of these remain. An earlier poem on Tristan had been written by a certain Beroul, but in this there was no allusion to Arthur. Here again the beginning points the way; Tristan, even in Malory, has never sat quite willingly at the Table. He is splendid and noble, but something always of an outland man. At Troyes Chrétien produced four poems—*Erec et Enide*, *Cligès*, *Lancelot*, *Yvain*; it is thought, in that order. He was presently at another court to produce another poem, *Perlesvaux*. All these poems take advantage of the superb background which had been provided. It was there for the using, and Chrétien chose to use it, and to do almost as much for it as his predecessor Geoffrey and his successor Robert. This applies especially to the *Lancelot*. But all four eulogize the great king. The *Erec* begins: 'In spring, at Easter, King Arthur held court at Cardigan', and proceeds with an adventure on which the king himself rides, the hunt of the White Hart. The *Cligès* says (after a paragraph or so): 'Alexander (the son of the Emperor at Byzantium—even he) had heard of King Arthur, who was reigning then, and of the chivalry who were about him, through whom he was honoured and feared in all parts of the world.' The *Lancelot* begins: 'On a certain day of the Ascension King Arthur had come from Caerleon and held a magnificent court at Camelot'; and the *Yvain*: 'That good King Arthur of Britain, from whom all of us learn constancy and courage, held once, upon that precious feast which is called Pentecost, a rich and royal court at Cardoal in Wales.' *Erec* contains a list of some of the lords. 'Gawaine should be named first of all that excelling chivalry; next was Erec, the son of Lac; and third, Lancelot of the Lake. Gornemant of Gohort was fourth; the Handsome Coward fifth. The sixth was the Ugly Brave, the seventh Maliant of Liz, the eighth Marduit the Wise, the ninth Didinel the Wild; and let Gardelen be called the tenth, for he was a goodly man.

I will name the rest as the names may come, for the numbers inconvenience me.' Some names among 'the rest' are of interest. Tristan was there, who never laughed; he sat beside Bliobleheris; Girflet the son of Do, who in the later Malory has become the rather shattering (because unexplained) Giroflet fils de Dieu; Loholt, 'the son of King Arthur, a youth of great merit', and Gronosis, 'versed in evil', the son of Kay the Seneschal—both these were to disappear entirely; King Lot, of whom no more is said. Besides these companions of the royal chivalry—the Round Table, of course, had not yet been invented —there were the dukes and kings whom King Arthur summoned to his court. There was Maheloas, 'a great baron, lord of the isle of Voirre, where no thunder is heard and no lightning strikes; there are no storms; no toads or serpents dwell in it; and it is never either too hot or too cold.' This sounds like the island of Avalon, but it is not, for the lord of Avalon was there too, Guigomar, a friend of Morgan the Fay. King Ban of Gornoret brought two hundred beardless young men, all carrying hawks; and King Kerrin of Riel three hundred white-bearded sages, of whom the youngest is sevenscore years old. There also was the King of the Antipodes, the smallest of all dwarfs. It is, here, a court almost as strange as that other which surrounded Solomon, son of David, king in Jerusalem, where angels and Afrits, and all the quarters of the world, came; though the Ring on his finger exercised a power over them which no property of King Arthur's ever had.

It will have been noticed that the first of the knights named is Gawaine, and this holds everywhere in Chrétien. Gawaine is the king's nephew, and is always treated as being next to the king. 'Welcome,' says a lady in *Yvain*, receiving the court, 'welcome a hundred thousand times to my lord the king, and blessed be his nephew, my lord Gawaine.' He is the most notable of all, and the only one who is permanently equal to the various different heroes of the poems. Lancelot, outside the poem named after him, is only mentioned twice; once in *Erec*, as above; and the second time in *Cligès*, where it is admitted that he does not lack courage but it is also said that if Cligès were dressed in a sack and Lancelot in silver and gold, Cligès would be the fairer. Lancelot is overthrown ; ' he could not help himself ; he gave himself up to Cligès '. But Cligès, of course, could not overcome Gawaine ; they fought equally, and the king had to make peace between them. Even in the *Lancelot* itself, Gawaine is ' the most admired and most famous knight upon whom ever the sign of the Cross was made '. He is the noble friend and champion of lesser knights. He is, in fact, exactly what the chief knight should be and what Lancelot was afterwards to become ; and one might think that Lancelot's first step towards it was when it was said of him, in his own particular poem, that ' Gawaine would not have cared to be king, if he could not have had Lancelot by his side '.

All these lords, if not first named in Chrétien, are first grouped and distinguished by him. But the real new power whom he brought into that assembly, the lord who up to now had hardly been named there, and had had no chance to be superbly tyrannical over the chivalry, was Love itself. Geoffrey of Monmouth had spoken of it. But now Love was to be the master as much as the king and Love the theme as much as war. It was, of course, a particular kind of Love ; Love as it appeared in that age and to the court of Troyes, enlivened by Chrétien's genius. It was ' courtly love '. On the other hand the reader who before looking at Chrétien has heard a good deal of this, its manners, its moralities and immoralities, its literature and its effects, may at first when he does look at Chrétien be a little surprised to find that it is not only real and recognizable but even respectable. The *Lancelot* may, for the moment, be excepted from this generalization. But the *Erec* depends upon a married relationship ; the whole question is of the effect of a state of settled love upon a man's proper activities. And in the *Cligès* marriage is twice stressed : the first time, by a general statement ; the second, by the details of the story.

In both poems the lovers examine themselves, in the literary manner of the day, upon this astonishing passion. They dilate on the effect that this Grand Master of body and mind has on them. They do not very much go into the soul ; there is nothing of Dante here, and nothing of what, after Dante had finished with it, has been meant by romantic love. This is the early style, and not yet mature. Soredamours, who is in love with Alexander, speaks to herself of her love :

'Shall I call him by his name or shall I call him friend ? Friend ? Not I ; but what then ? the name of friend is fair and sweet to speak. . . . He would not lie if he were to call me his sweet friend. And should I if I spoke so to him ? . . . If I spoke his name, I should be afraid of stumbling in the middle ; but " friend "—I could soon speak that short word. I would be willing to shed my blood if his name were simply " my sweet friend ".'

It is Guinevere who brings the lovers together. She causes them to be called to her and addresses them.

'Alexander, love is worse than hate when it torments its devotees. Lovers do not know what they are doing when they hide from each other their passion. Love is a serious business, and whoever is not bold enough to lay the foundation properly will never be able to finish the building. Both of you are acting foolishly in maintaining this silence ; concealment will kill you, and then you will have murdered Love. Now my counsel to you is to put no tyranny and to seek no temporary delight in Love, but to be joined together in all honour in marriage ; thus Love will, I believe, endure a great while. Do but agree, and I will take it on myself to arrange the marriage.'

Alexander answers that, if he had dared, he would have spoken long ago ; silence has indeed been hard. 'But it may be that this maid does not choose to be mine or that I should be hers. Even then, though she does not give me the right, I will put myself in her hands.' Soredamours answers falteringly that she is—all of her, will, heart, and body—at the disposal of the queen. Guinevere laughs, embraces them, and says : 'I give each one of you to the other. Take, Soredamours, what is yours, and you, Alexander, what is yours.'

The queen here is something nobler than the barely visible

Guanhumara and than she who loved Lanval. There is in her a touch of the Guinevere she was to become, she who in Malory said to the court, at the first appearance of Galahad : ' I may well suppose that Sir Lancelot begat him on King Pelles' daughter, by the which he was made to lie, by enchantment, and his name is Galahad. I would fain see him, said the queen, for he must needs be a noble man, for so is his father that him begat ; I report me unto all the Table Round.' It is true she was there speaking outside marriage, and yet perhaps not, for it would be improper to assume that the queen was not as much in love with the nobility of Lancelot as with his person ; and if his person some-times dominated his nobility in her, the realism is truer so. But the development of that royal figure must be left till a later chapter. But the main point is her reference to marriage ; it is thus that Love is to be built and thus that it is to endure. Whatever other poets did, whatever in another poem Chrétien himself did, here the paramount opportunity and privilege of marriage is laid down. In the second part of the poem, which deals with the adventures of Alexander's son Cligès, marriage is safeguarded by the details. Alexander's brother Alis has seized the imperial throne. Alexander consents to leave him in peace, provided he swears not to marry, which he does. But after Alexander's death, he breaks his oath and proceeds to espouse and to marry Fénice, the daughter of the Emperor of the West. The marriage is thus null and void from the beginning. Fénice is, of course, in love with Cligès, and he with her. But they conceal it, ' There was no eye so keen nor ear so sharp as to gather from anything seen or heard that there was love between those two.' Cligès leaves for Britain and King Arthur ; Fénice for Byzantium. There her nurse makes a drink for the Emperor by which he falls into illusion, and dreams that he has his pleasure with Fénice, while she lies safe by his side, ' as if there were a wall between them '. It is a magical preservation of her virginity, but it is meant to be justified by the Emperor's perjury. Cligès returns and entreats Fénice to escape with him. But she will not do it so. ' Everyone,' she says, ' when we had gone, would speak evil of our love; they would not believe the truth; indeed, they could not. They would talk of us as if we were Tristan and Iseult the Fair.' It has been said of this that she is merely being anxious about her reputation, but this is hardly fair. She quotes St. Paul; she is anxious not to give scandal. Our own age has largely lost that fear, perhaps because we are sensitive to the other danger of hypocrisy, so that we have come to think that sin loses half its evil by losing all its secrecy, unless for personal reasons of kindness. But this is hardly so; and scandal, it seems, was to Chrétien a very real harm. If she could be thought dead . . . and by the help of another potion she arranges to be thought dead, in spite of incredible tortures by rods and by melted lead applied by the doctors. She suffers all this—for her reputation? say rather, for her love and for what she thought the common good. An empress, even an un-canonical empress, must not be generally thought to have run off with her lover. Eventually her device succeeds, though she is afterwards discovered and compelled after all to escape with Cligès to King Arthur. Cligès makes ' claim and protest to the king that his uncle the emperor had disloyally taken a wife, when he had sworn he would never marry all his life. And the king answered that he would gather a thousand ships and fill them with knights, and three thousand with men-at-arms, so that no city or borough, town or castle, could resist him, and with this fleet he will set out for Byzantium '. This is the judgement of Arthur, the master of courtesy and chivalry. But news comes that the emperor is dead, and the lovers return to reign. ' And Cligès still called his wife mistress and love, and she had no loss of love to complain of, for he loved her always as his lady, and she him as her lover, and every day their love grew stronger.' Which was what the queen Guinevere had promised his father.

It is true that in the *Lancelot* there is a difference. This is a story of an abduction of Guinevere. Sir Edmund Chambers has said that ' as the schoolgirl wrote, she was a lady very much subject to the misfortune of being run away with '. It might be urged on her behalf that the poets and romancers could think of very little else for her to do or be. They had refused her a family. Loholt, the son of Arthur, made an appearance in *Erec*, but he was killed off in Chrétien's own later poem, *Perlesvaux*, and I doubt if (since then) anyone except Sir Walter Scott has been daring enough to imagine an heir to Arthur. Wace indeed had lamented that he was ' a childless man ', with ' the sorer sorrow '. Her lovers were always leaving her, to ride out on quests, ' for fear of their reputation '. The king, except here and there, is never shown to have any great interest in her nor she in him, though they appear together superbly in public. Until the tragic shock of the close was invented, she was not allowed to have a concern for religion, nor (more oddly, perhaps, considering everything) was she allowed to form such a court of love and poetry as seems to have existed at Troyes. No ; she had little to do but to be abducted and to be rescued, until her poets filled her empty life with Lancelot.

But in the poem of that name she is not yet fully herself. She is carried away by Meleagaunt to the country of his father King Bagdemagus. This country is clearly derived from one of those lands of the dead made familiar in more ancient tales. But in the poem of Troyes it is not allowed to have its terrifying identity ; only in glimpses can we catch sight of its original nature, through the ordered process of the love-tale. In the hither province of Bagdemagus's country are many of the people of the land of Logres who are held captive there ' by the custom of the land '. ' No stranger enters this land but he is compelled to stay.' He is not imprisoned in the ordinary sense ; he may be free and rich. But he can never again cross the frontier back to Logres. After this, something more than mere adventure seems to hide in the account of the two bridges ; the one under water, and as much water above as below ; the other, the edge of a sharp sword, as long as two lances. It is here that the name of Logres seems to be first used for King Arthur's land ; its derivation is said to be from the Welsh Lloegr, a land of faerie which was also Britain or within Britain. But none of these things are developed by Chrétien ; they only strike the reader suddenly with something more like a faint terror than the other tales of the king have anywhere suggested. Mr. C. S. Lewis has said that ' it is one of Chrétien's misfortunes that the dark and tremendous suggestions of the Celtic myth that lurk in the background of his story should so far (for a modern reader) overshadow the love and adventure of the foreground '. But then the Middle Ages were, to themselves, modern.

It was to the foreground that Chrétien attended, and the foreground in the *Lancelot* (much more than in the other poems) was courtly love, love as it was talked and sung and even practised in courts. Courts in that century had, like so many things, a freedom they had not long possessed ; there was room and time to be refined, and codes by which to be refined. In Provence they had refined love into a code, and through Europe the men and women of the courts copied Provence. It may, however, be added that in some respects at least Provence had first copied life. Some of our modern discussions on courtly love seem to begin by removing it wholly from human experience. It was, no doubt, a separation and an exaggeration of what was at best only one element in human experience, and at its worst it became, no doubt, as all such separations and exaggerations will, a false caricature of even that element. People in whom it hardly existed at all had to pretend not only that it existed, but that practically nothing else existed. Something of the same overstrained effort was true of Geneva under Calvin and is all but true of England under democracy. But that does not alter the fact that the democratic effort is part of the English experience, that the Will of God was a very serious part of the experience of many holy souls in Geneva, and that the code of courtly love expressed a particular kind of passion felt by many lovers then and now. Thus the *Lancelot* said of its hero that he knelt to the queen, ' for in no holy body had he such belief '. The physical beauty of Guinevere appeared to him a thing literally transcendental. This is, no doubt, what the code told him he ought to feel and in any case how he ought to behave. It

will not do, however, to forget that a great number of lovers
have felt like this. To codify—almost to institutionalize—is
perhaps unwise, but the folly (if it is a folly) does not abolish
the original reality; any more than the imbecilities of some of
the disciples of Wordsworth about flowers and mountains alter
the fact that Wordsworth and many others have been moved
and exalted by flowers and mountains. The body of the beloved
appears vital with holiness; the physical flesh is glorious with
sanctity—not her sanctity, but its own. It is gay and natural to
genuflect to it. Such an experience may exist before marriage,
in marriage, and after marriage; it is the *stupor* of which Dante
wrote and which we, when we read of it, immediately recognize.
The code was, no doubt, an invention, but not the passion that
caused the code. That it sometimes led—and leads—to adultery
no more disproves its validity than the fact that it may lead to
marriage or renunciation proves it. It may be a temptation,
exactly as Isabella in *Measure for Measure* was a temptation to
Angelo. But it would seem difficult to deny the apparent
enskying and sainting of Isabella merely because Angelo was
tempted by it.

But at this time the whole of this particular experience was
separated, arranged, codified, and to a large extent falsified in
the process. It was also made fashionable and falsified still
further. In Chrétien's *Lancelot* one can almost see the thing
happening. Geoffrey of Monmouth had alluded to that love in
the king's court which encouraged all lovers to virtue, but he
had not gone into the matter. Wace had said that the king and
his knighthood were Love's lovers, but he too had contented
himself with the suggestion of a general glow of bright affection.
It is a part of the whole glory; it is neither made very particular
in itself, nor is it particularized in any of the personages. It is
more in the nature of the masculine companionship than markedly
between men and women; that, at least, is the kind of love that
dominates. The king, when he hears of the death of Gawaine,
is said to feel a special grief: ' there too was Gawaine his nephew
killed; and Arthur made great sorrow over him; for this

knight was dearer to him than any other man'. But the only peer of Arthur, so far, who is allowed to have any love-interest is Mordred, and it is in general rather the queen, the king's wife, rather than the woman, his own lady, whom he seizes and marries. The deed is political rather than amorous. Love, however, was now to enter the court, and Love was to be, then and there, courtly love. Lancelot was, apparently by Chrétien's choice or by that of his patron, the Countess of Champagne, to be presented in that kind as the proper and perfect lover. But his refined perfection is not wholly alien.

The most famous incident of his career, after that manner and in this poem, is that of the cart; from which afterwards a prose version of the poem derived its name, *La Conte de la Charette*. It comes close to the original abduction of the queen. Lancelot followed, and after him Gawaine. Lancelot lost his horse, apparently in a battle with Meleagaunt, and presently overtook a cart driven by a dwarf. Now at that time a cart was a rare thing, and evil. There was only one in each town, and it was used to expose and carry to execution, thieves, murderers, traitors, and other criminals. Anyone who had been carried in a cart lost all reputation and legal right; he was dead in law, and could no more show himself in courts or towns. Anyone who met a cart crossed himself and said a prayer. It is possible that this is not without some relation to the queen being carried to the kingdom of the dead; at least, that relation obviously proposes itself to us, though Chrétien has not much use for it. Lancelot asked the dwarf for news of the queen; the dwarf answered that if the knight would mount the cart, he should presently hear of her. For a couple of steps Lancelot hesitated. Reason and Love dispute, for that time, within him. Reason loses; Love triumphs; he climbs in. Presently, when he had undergone many adventures, and crossed the sword-bridge, and overcome Meleagaunt, he was brought by Bagdemagus to the queen, whom he had now liberated. But she had heard of his hesitation. She threw him a cold look and would not speak to him. Lancelot, ' feeling very helpless ' (how one's heart leaps at that phrase ! how one recognizes the chilly glance, the silent mouth !), decided that his fault must be in having ridden in the cart at all. This, of course, is exactly what a man would think, and might even sometimes be quite right in thinking ; one never quite knows which way the admirable feminine mind will spring. He was wrong; his fault lay only in his delay. Presently, after an alarm of death on both sides, she softened. He dared to ask how he had offended her. She answered : ' You must remember that you were not at all in a hurry to get in that cart ; you went two good steps before you did.' Lancelot abased himself profoundly. ' For God's sake, lady, take my amends, and tell me if you can forgive me.' The queen said : ' Willingly ; I forgive you entirely.'

No doubt this is an extreme example of courtly love. But no doubt also it is based on general human experience. The delay in action may, to a woman, mean more than the action itself. ' I'm not convinced by proofs but signs ' says Patmore's young woman ; and all masculine heroism without feminine tact is apt to go wrong. Where one expected gratitude (not that Lancelot did) one finds austerity. Oh perhaps the Provençals manipulated love too much, but undoubtedly they knew what they were manipulating !

Lancelot ' loved more than Pyramus, if that were possible '. On one occasion he and ' a damsel ' found near a spring a comb of gilded ivory in which golden hairs were tangled. The girl said she was sure it belonged to the queen. ' " There are many kings and queens ; which do you mean ? " " Fair lord, I speak of King Arthur's wife." ' Lancelot, at the sudden sentence, all but fainted (a Provençal lover ; but it happens outside Provence ; he is not perhaps so fortunate who has never felt his colour change at such an unexpected pang). He keeps the hair—' he despises essence of pearl, treacle, and the cure for pleurisy ; he does not need St. Martin or St. James ; he puts such great trust in this hair.' So the handkerchief of the beloved in its degree is sometimes much like the Veronican ; the face of Love is there.

On the other hand when, at a tournament, Lancelot on the

first day triumphed, and the queen on the second sent him word he was to do his worst, he obeyed, for he did not mind being thought cowardly, so only that he did his lady's will—it is then almost impossible not to feel that the convention is being pressed beyond likelihood ; or if it is not, that the likelihood of that age is indeed different from ours. A woman—even a queen—ought not so to interfere in a man's business. It may be that one ought to stop fighting—or writing a poem or doing excavations—if one's lady wishes, but that she should bid one fight badly or write a poor poem or do silly excavations : this even Love can hardly command. Reason has a word to say. Alas, if Reason had, in that day Reason lost. It is not the smallest advantage of the divine Dante a century and a half later that he believed Love to aid Reason ' in all things proper to Reason '. But then the image of Beatrice was ' of so noble a virtue ' that it is impossible to imagine her commanding her lover to write a bad poem for her sole whim. There is something about Guinevere—even Malory's Guinevere—which does not make it quite impossible for her. It is a little perhaps because, until the end, she is never shown to us in a moral distress over her marriage and her love. She might have been sinful, but she should have been troubled ; not being, she remains faintly more egotistic than high literature allows.

In the *Lancelot* there is no doubt about the love affair. When they were reconciled Lancelot came to the queen by night. In order to enter her room he had to bend and wrench out the bars of the window and in doing so he cut his fingers. He did not notice it, so intent was he on the queen. In the morning ' his body goes and his heart stays ; yet his body so far stays that the blood which has fallen from his fingers stains the queen's bed '. He straightened the bars behind him ; then he bowed towards the room as if towards a shrine. The two elements of a proper worship and (*pace* the adultery) a proper sensuality are too close together for our taste. The maxim for any love affair is ' Play and pray ; but on the whole do not pray when you are playing and do not play when you are praying.' We cannot yet manage such simultaneities, and it is difficult for us to believe that the early Middle Ages could. A formal genuflection may be all that is meant, but even that—then and there—is distasteful.

However this may be, the *Lancelot* is the first statement of the love between Lancelot and the queen. It is also, so to speak, the promotion of Lancelot. Gawaine, who had followed him, but had not been much use, rebuked those at Arthur's court who praised him. ' " These honours are shameful to me, for I did not reach the queen in time to free her. But Lancelot was there in time and won such honour as was never won by any other knight." ' This, as one might say, settled the matter not only in the poem, but outside the poem. If the queen was to be loved and rescued it was Lancelot who was to do it. If Lancelot was to do it, and to be the queen's lover, he was to become more and more important. Subject to the genius of future poets, he must become in fact the rival—in some sense, the equal—of the king. To make a proper relationahip, he and the king must each in turn outgrow the other. At the moment when Lancelot bent and pulled the bars of the window of the queen's room, it was determined that, for all the courtly conventions in which it was begun, it was to be a business of sensuality as well as of adoration. Unless any greater genius interfered with that development, the sensual passion would be likely to grow. No greater genius did. ' So fair, so bold, so serene ', the king Bagdemagus called Lancelot ; these qualities, but shaken, troubled, and darkened by that unhappy and indulged passion were to be with him to the end. Love had indeed come to the court of Arthur, and presently a ruin beyond the dreams of courtly love was to follow it.

CHAPTER V

The Coming of the Grail

THE last poem written by Chrétien de Troyes is the first
European poem in which an object called 'a grail' certainly
appears. The poem was in fact originally called *Le Conte du
Graal* ; afterwards it became known as *Perceval*. It was written,
Chrétien says, at the suggestion of Philip, Count of Flanders, to
whose court the poet had apparently transferred himself, and
'from a book which the Count gave me'. The Count is known
to have left Flanders for the Holy Land in 1190 and died there
in 1191. Chrétien is thought to have been engaged on the poem
a little earlier, between 1174 and 1180, and to have died before
he had finished it. It was then taken up by other writers, and
Chrétien's original 10,000 lines were expanded to over 60,000.
In these continuations the original grail underwent development ;
it became particular and the grand material object of Christian
myth.

A second group of poems—meant as one—took up the subject.
They were written by Robert de Borron. There were three of
these poems, of which two remain : *Joseph d'Arimathie*, *Merlin*,
and a *Perceval* known to us only in a later prose version. De
Borron was a client of Gautier de Montbeliard, at whose request
the poem was composed. Gautier too left France ; in 1199 he
was in Italy ; in 1201 in Palestine. There he became Constable
of Jerusalem. It will be remembered that the Pope Urban II
had proclaimed the First Crusade in 1095 and that from then
onwards for a couple of centuries the thought of the liberation
of the Holy Places occupied a definite place in the imagination
of Western Europe. The word 'liberation' is useful here,
because we have ourselves known it. It was no more the only
cause of the Crusades than the liberation of Europe was the only
cause of our own war. Self-preservation—physical and econ-

omical—from that threatening mass of Islam came in—as a similar preservation did with us. But as that other thought moved seriously and widely among us, so with them. It would be as false to say that they did not think of Jerusalem as that we did not think of Paris. Jerusalem was recovered for the West (to which it was always considered to belong) in 1099. In 1187 it was again captured by Saladin. The three chief lords of the West—Philip Augustus King of France, Richard Plantagenet King of England, Frederick Barbarossa the Emperor in the West —moved to free it. It was under the continuous impulse of this desire for liberation that the Count of Flanders and the lord of Montbeliard moved—the latter certainly in connexion with that spectacular Third Crusade. It is true it failed ; the title of Constable of Jerusalem was a vain brag or a deliberate challenge. But it was not known that it would fail.

There were, therefore, in that twelfth century, two influences of this realistic kind on Chrétien and de Borron. The first was the conversation, referred to in the first chapter, on the Blessed Sacrament which was conducted among the intellectuals, among the semi-intellectuals, and among the pseudo-intellectuals. It was not, of course, supposed to be a conversation on an unimportant point of theology ; it was a discussion on something that was going on in every parish in Europe. The second influence was the general idea of the crusades for the Holy Places. Abandon the disputes and the wars, and it still remains true that the thought of the Eucharist and the thought of Jerusalem were in the minds of most men. They were, then, the modern subjects, and the poets and romancers treated them in their own modern way. Chrétien declares that his story is ' the best tale that has ever been told in royal courts '. De Borron says that until he wrote ' the great history of the Holy Grail had never been treated by mortal man '.

This sense of a living, exciting, and topical subject is still prominent in the early part of the next century, which was the period of the great prose romances. These were partly prose versions of the poems and partly new compositions. There were brought to bear on the subject a number of fresh romantic intelligences, whose names are unknown to us. They altered ; they enlarged ; they invented. They saw the opportunities their predecessors had missed ; and peculiarly they saw one opportunity—they devised a mythically satisfying Achievement of the Grail ; and eventually they brought the whole together in one great work, consisting (as one may say) of five parts—*L'Estoire du Saint Graal, L'Estoire de Merlin, L'Estoire de Lancelot, La Queste del Saint Graal*, and *Le Mort d'Artu*. This great achievement—in a literary sense—of the Grail is held to have been mainly concluded by 1230. And the important thing about it is that it was a literary achievement. It is occasionally forgotten, or seems to be, in the great scholarly discussions, that anyone who is writing a poem or a romance is primarily writing a poem or a romance. He will, of course, be affected, as the Crusaders in their task were affected, by all sorts of other things—his religious views, his political views, his need of money, the necessity for haste, the instructions of a patron, carelessness, forgetfulness, foolishness. But he is primarily concerned with making a satisfactory book. He may borrow anything from anywhere—if he thinks it makes a better book. He may leave out anything from anywhere—if he thinks it makes a better book. And this (it can hardly be doubted), rather than anything else, was the first cause of the invention of the glorious and sacred figure of Galahad.

It is impossible, and (were it possible) undesirable, in this volume to go in any but the briefest way into the many variations of the myth which lie between the *Conte du Graal* and the *Queste del Saint Graal*, or into the complex questions of date, origin, and relationship. They all lie behind Malory, and it is Malory's book which is for English readers the record book of Arthur and of the Grail. It is, however, permissible to note a few of the points of development. We may say that there were [five] [1] of them :

(i) The determination of the Grail as a subject, and the invention of its history.

[1] I have supplied this word : the MS. has a blank space. [C. S. L.]

(ii) The relation of this—at first generally ; then definitely through Merlin—with the figure of King Arthur.

(iii) The invention of the Dolorous Blow.

(iv) The development of the love of Lancelot and Guinevere.

(v) The invention of Galahad.

(i) Chrétien's *Conte du Graal* dealt with the adventure of a youth named Perceval, afterwards Perceval le Gallois, or Perceval of Wales. He was the son of a widow who wished to keep him with her at home. But he met by chance certain knights of King Arthur's court, whom he questioned. Excited by this, he determined to go to the court and there achieve knighthood. He set out ; as he went, he looked back and saw his mother fall to the ground, fainting with grief. He would not return ; he went on, and came to the court where (after the usual difficult episode with Sir Kay, who was becoming the most churlish of all the lords) he went off in pursuit of a Red Knight, by killing whom he supplied himself with armour. He then remained for some time with an old knight, Gournemant, who taught him the usage of chivalry and eventually knighted him, giving him three pieces of advice—to be slow to speak, to be slow to ask questions, and to be slow to quote his mother's sayings on all occasions. He then came to the town and castle of Beaurepair where Gournemant's niece Blanchfleur lived. She was threatened by an evil king and asked Perceval's help. After the two young people had spent the night together, Perceval overthrew the king, sent him to Arthur, and presently departed. He came to a river where two men were fishing from a boat. One of them directed him to a castle close by. There Perceval was taken into the hall, where were four hundred men sitting round a fire, and an old man lying on a couch. The old man gave him a sword on which was an inscription that it will break only in one peril, and that known only to the maker. Presently a squire entered, bearing a lance from the point of which a drop of blood continually ran down ; then came two more squires, each carrying a ten-branched candlestick ; and after them a damsel bearing ' a grail '. What the grail was is not defined ; only it is said that the light which shone from it wholly abolished the blaze of the candles which preceded it. After it came another damsel carrying a silver plate. The pageant passed between the couch and the fire and went out. Perceval, remembering Gournemant's advice, did not venture to ask any question. Supper was served in the hall, and with each course the grail was brought in and carried to an inner room where some unknown person was fed with a Host from it. Perceval still asked nothing. He was taken to his chamber ; the next morning he found the castle deserted and his horse waiting, ready saddled, outside it. Riding away, he presently came to a place where a knight was lying dead and a girl weeping over him. It was from her that he now learnt that the Fisherman and the old man of the castle were the same person—a king who had been mysteriously wounded by a spear through the thigh. If only (she went on) Perceval had asked what was the meaning of the pageant he had seen; the king would have been healed and the land should have had great good. She also told him that his mother was dead, and that he was responsible, for she had died from sorrow at his departure. Later in the poem this is confirmed by a hermit who is Perceval's uncle and adds that Perceval is in a state of sin because of his mother's death ; it is this sin which prevented him asking the question. After this the poem involved itself— as far as Chrétien went—with adventures of Perceval, Gawaine, and others which have no immediately significant connexion with the Grail.

Here then are the earlier images—the strange castle, the wounded king, the sword, the bleeding lance, the grail, the mysterious nourishment, the unasked question, and the consequent lack of some great good. There is, in the unfinished poem, no attempt at explanation. But there are three critical comments to be made. The first is simply that the wound in the thighs is primarily a wound in the thighs. It is, no doubt, being in the thighs, symbolical of sex or fertility or anything else of that sort. But at least it is a wound which has got to be somehow explained.

The explanation, if we had had it, might have been as unsatis-
factory as many of the explanations in the Elizabethan drama.
But the story, unless it were to drop the Wounded King altogether, had got to deal with it. It may be added that if we
assume that Chrétien and his successors thought the thighs
symbolical of sex, they may have thought sex itself symbolical.
Or (to put it less in our modern phrases) that if the wound was
to be a wound in virility, it was to be a wound in the whole
virility, spiritual as well as physical. We must not force his
imagination so far as to say he did, but we can hardly limit it
so far as to say he did not. If it were not he, but we, who add
the interpretation, then again we should be prepared to take it
in its fullest sense.

(ii) The second comment refers to the lance and the grail.
Where Chrétien got these from, or whether he got them from
anywhere, we do not know. What seems to be true is that these
two things are different in kind from what preceded them.
There had been (the scholars tell us) Celtic lances that flamed,
but there was no Celtic lance that bled. There had been (they
also tell us) vessels and cauldrons which produced physical food ;
but the grail in Chrétien did not produce physical food. The
whole and exact point of its use was that it provided a substitute
for physical food. Perceval and the knights and the Fisher King
are served with supper ; but the question Perceval did not ask
was : ' What serves the Grail ? ' It served an unknown per-
sonage with a Host ; if it was like anything, it was like the
ciborium of the Eucharist, and contained the super-substantial
food.

(iii) The third point is no more than the suggestion of a possibility. It will be remarked that there were two reasons given
for Perceval's failure to ask the question : (i) the advice of
Gournemant, (ii) his state of sin consequent on his treatment of
his mother. It a little looks as if Chrétien, in writing, had felt
that the first was inadequate and had strengthened it by the
second. A question of such importance, it might be held, ought
to have been prevented by some matter more grave than the

misapplication of an old man's maxims.   It is, of course, possible
that the first reason was that which Perceval's conscious mind
supplied and that the second—the sense of guilt precluding an
enquiry into apparent sanctity—was the real motive, and that
Chrétien meant it so.   He would not have talked in those terms
but he need not have been ignorant of such facts.   The main
point is that Perceval's respect for Gournemant is too small a
cause for so heavy a result, even allowing that Gournemant was
Perceval's father in chivalry, to whom special honour was owed.
But the death of the lady his mother is due to a breach in a filial
relationship of blood and not of knighthood ; he has shown a
callous impatience in not returning when he saw her swoon.
However proper his impulse to go, it is credible that the manner
of it should involve him in sin ; and it is certainly credible that,
being so involved, he should not be able to ask concerning a
holy thing.   There is the first faint hint—it is no more and is
probably unintentional—of a natural but unhallowed impulse
which fails before holiness.

The poets who followed and continued Chrétien took full
advantage of his themes.   All that is necessary here is to relate
certain things in them to the development of the myth as it
later crossed into England and became known to the general
reader.

(i) The first of these is the nature of the vessel itself.   In the
continuation the indefinite article is changed to the definite.   ' A
grail ' becomes ' the Grail ' and presently ' le Saint Graal ' or
' the Holy Grail '.   It is said in so many words to be that which
received the blood of Christ when he was on the cross, and the
Bleeding Lance is said to be the spear of the centurion Longinus
which he thrust into the side of Christ.   These identifications
mean that the Sacred Body enters into and becomes a part of
the tale.   It is not, at present, much more ; there are hardly any
theological attributions.   But poetically there is now a union
and a centre—not so much a Christian centre as an artistic.
From this poetic point of view, the whole development of the
myth is a kind of working out of a theme which is eventually

discovered to be the Christian theme. The centurion was extremely convenient; there he was, complete with spear and action. It is obvious that he was a poetic gift; he had not yet been used, and no poet (once the episode had occurred to him) could think of neglecting him. The general decision of scholars seems to be that none of the Continuators are likely to have had more than plain narrative in mind. But even plain narrative is the better for the unifying and heightening of its images. The Grail, therefore, was identified; it was also released. It was seen, or rather that light more than many candles which accompanied it, was seen outside the castle. Perceval sees it by night in that vast and ancient forest which surrounds the high cities of the myth; it is carried by its maiden or by an angel. It moves in Logres at the will of its keepers—or perhaps at its own will, but I think this has not yet happened. All of this, however, is a preparation for the later time when, in the English Malory, it was to be seen at Pentecost, veiled, before all the Table. It is also for the healing of wounds; when Perceval has fought with Sir Ector, it heals them both. On the other hand, it cannot— or at least does not—heal the Wounded Fisher-King. Nor does it restore fertility to the land outside the castle. In Chrétien this is not yet waste; only through Perceval's silence, some great good that might have come to it does not come. In the continuations, however, the land is already sterile, and the Grail does not restore it without that human initiative which the question implies. The holy thing ('chose espirituelle') cannot or will not nourish either its keeper or the earth until the called and choosing knight is there.

(ii) But even when the waste land had been supplied, and therefore the great good defined, the cause of the sterility and of the wound of the Fisher-King was still lacking. The important invention here was the first hint of the Dolorous Blow. In one of the continuations Perceval does ask the question, but no healing immediately follows. The Fisher-King tells him that he has been wounded by a sword (not, here, a spear) that has also slain his brother; he can only be healed when the murderer himself has been killed. In fact Perceval presently does slay the murderer and brings his head to the castle, whereupon the king, with a great cry, is made whole. But neither the original blow nor the healing seem yet related directly to the Grail. As for the sword which struck the blow, this is one of the various strange swords which wander in and out of the tale, but again without any apparent direct relation to the central Hallows. There is no need to follow them here ; there is a possible relation, but that can be better discussed later. Perceval left the castle and returned to the court of King Arthur. In one continuation, however, he was called back. The Grail-bearing maiden herself came to the court and told him that the Fisher-King was dead. He had been said to be another uncle of Perceval, so that by now Perceval himself has been raised to be part of the dynasty entrusted with the Guardianship and his relations are hermits and strange wardens. Perceval set out for the castle, but this time the king himself and all the chivalry accompanied him. It is but an episode in one poem, but prophetic of what is happening to the myth. The great Arthurian tradition is already beginning to move towards this other centre. On the Feast of All Saints Perceval was crowned king. King Arthur and the lords remained for a month in the castle where, under the influence of the Grail, they were fed with the richest food. Nothing more is heard of that other more ancient king who was in seclusion and fed only by the Host. King Arthur returned to Britain or Logres, and Perceval reigned for seven years. After that time he left the castle for a hermitage where the Hallows accompanied him. There he was after five years made a priest, and there, fed by the Grail—but now spiritually—he remained till he died. This was afterwards to remain his end in the myth ; after the ascension of Galahad, ' Sir Percivale ', says Malory, ' yielded him to a hermitage out of the city, and took a religious clothing. . . . Thus a year and two months lived Sir Percivale in the hermitage a full holy life, and then passed out of this world ; and Bors let bury him by his sister and by Galahad in the spiritualities.'

(iii) The mention of ' his sister ' raises another point—of the women related to Perceval in the beginnings. There are three, Blanchfleur and the Lady of the Chessboard and his sister. Blanchfleur was the young chatelaine of Beaurepair, the niece of Gournemant, whom he had delivered from her enemy and with whom for a night he had slept. It was a sleep of betrothal rather than of casualness ; they promised marriage in the morning, and are bound. But after that—in one poem—he had a strange adventure in a castle where he played chess with an invisible opponent and met a lady who promised him her love if he would kill a certain stag (the chase of such a stag by one or other champion is a common episode). Eventually he did so, and returned to take his pleasure with the lady. But in another continuation, which does not trouble about the chessboard, it was Blanchfleur to whom he returned in the end, but they proposed to themselves, though they lay side by side, to indulge no intercourse with each other until the adventures of the Grail were ended. There came, however, presently a voice from heaven which encouraged them not to abandon their ' delit carnel ', and prophesied that from that marriage should spring Godfrey of Bouillon, the conqueror of Jerusalem.[1]

But this dedication obviously puts Blanchfleur in at least indirect relation with the Grail. Unfortunately at that point she disappears from the story for the time. She is, however, by now a kind of assistant in the grand adventure, as is the third lady his sister. No sister had been heard of in Chrétien ; the only lady there of Perceval's kin was his mother. But in one of the continuations he returns to his mother's house and there finds his sister, ' blanc cum floure en may novele '. She visits with him the hermit-uncle ; they pray together ; they hear a Mass of the Holy Ghost. He is encouraged and commanded to the adventure. It is to be feared that the Lady of the Chessboard ruined Perceval's chances—but perhaps they were not high—of being the final Grail hero, for reasons which we shall see. One cannot wholly separate a mythical hero from his past in the myth.

[1] Also the Swan Knight of another tale, but he cannot be followed here. [C. W.]

But there remained that figure of sanctity, feminine and self-giving, ' une sainte chose', who in Malory gave her blood for another and whose dead body was carried to the final achievement on the deck of that ship where were Bors, and Percivale and Galahad—to be buried in ' the spiritual places'.

It may be remarked that in these poems Gawaine plays a part, but never much of a part as regards the Grail. He does reach the castle, but he falls asleep there ; he is a great lord, but he had been (I suspect) too much a great lord of the court. Something simpler and stranger was needed. The result, however, was that, as the court and the Grail drew together, Gawaine lost place. He had no intense relation either to the Sacred Body or to the body of the queen.

But all these developments and variations left one part of the myth yet untold—the early history of the holy thing. De Borron set out to supply this ; he said he had it ' from the great book in which are the histories told by the grand clerks ; there the mighty secrets are written which are named and called the Grail '. Some account of this part of the tale must be given here.

After the arrest of Christ, the vessel in which he made his sacrament—' ou Criz faisoit son sacrament ', ' la senefiance de ma mort '—was found in the house and taken to Pilate. Pilate, wishing to be free from all connexion with him, gave it to Joseph of Arimathea at the time he came to beg the Sacred Body. When the Body was taken from the Cross and bathed, the wounds began again to bleed. Joseph caught the blood in the vessel and hid it in his own house, as he did the body in the tomb. After the harrowing of hell and the resurrection, Joseph was seized and imprisoned by the Jews in a tall tower which could be entered only from the top. There our Lord appeared to him, himself bringing the Grail, from which light shone, and deigned to declare himself concerning it. It is to have three keepers ; all who see it will be of the Lord's own company, and shall have the desire of their hearts, and perdurable joy ; those who can understand these words will not, if they are true men, ever be defrauded or falsely judged in any court or defeated in ordeal of battle. The sacrament will never be celebrated without recollection of Joseph, because of the tenderness and care he has shown for the body of Christ ; and in those celebrations the elements will be indeed his flesh and blood ; [1] the cup will represent the Grail and be called a chalice ; the altar is the tomb ; the corporal the grave clothes ; the paten the stone at the mouth of the tomb. There is then communicated to Joseph the secret which is the Grail. Christ leaves the actual Grail with him and vanishes. Joseph remained in prison for forty years, fed by the sacred vessel.

At the end of that time the Emperor of Rome and his son Vespasian come to Jerusalem. Vespasian had been a leper and had been healed by the handkerchief of Veronica. He and his father intended to avenge the death of Christ ; and Vespasian himself, on hearing of Joseph from the Jews, descended into the tower and set the prisoner free. Once released, Joseph gathered a company of believers round him and set out on a great journey ; among them were his sister Enygeus and her husband Hebron or Bron. They travelled a long distance to the west ; but presently they settled in a certain district and gave themselves to prayer and the cultivation of the earth. Some of them, however, fell into sin, and the land itself began to become sterile. Joseph prayed before the Grail for direction, and a voice from the Holy Ghost told him what he must do.

He made, at these commands, a great table, such as that was at which Christ made the significance of his death. One seat was to be drawn back from it, in memory of Judas, and left unfilled until the son of Bron should at some future time sit there. Bron was sent to catch a fish and it was laid on the table, where also the Grail was set, but covered. The whole company were called in and invited to sit down. Some did, but some did not. Those who did were filled with a divine sweetness ; they experienced the satisfaction of all desire. Those

[1] It will be remembered that He was—and is—believed to be received perfect and entire under either species. [C. W.]

71

who could not sit felt nothing; these were the sinners. These were sent away, but one of them, Moyses, after many entreaties, made an effort to sit down in the withdrawn and perilous chair. The earth at once opened and swallowed him; there, the sacred voice proclaimed, he must be left until he who was meant for the chair shall come. This was the wrath of the Grail.

Presently the true company were given more commands. Bron and his wife had twelve children, of whom the youngest Alain was to be the father of another Alain, who should become the third keeper of the Grail. The second was to be Bron himself, and it was now the time for the Grail to be delivered to him. Alain was sent away with a part of the company to preach Christ among the heathen. But Joseph in a high ceremony gave the holy vessel into the guardianship of Bron, who by divine instruction was henceforth to be called the Rich Fisher; to him also the secrets were communicated. The Fisher also went on with the rest of the company, carrying the Grail and passing to the West. But there, wherever he chose, he might remain until his son's son should come—to whom the vessel and the grace should pass. Arimathean Joseph remained in his own land, celestially blest. The mystery that lies behind all is his care for that arch-natural Body, when he took it from the cross. It is that deposition which, in some sense, governs all the myth; and this which lies behind the future rejection of Lancelot. It was for that reason that there had been made known to Joseph in his prison ' the holy words, sweet and precious, gracious and pitiful, which are called the Secret of the Grail '. It is added, in the prose version, that those who hear are entreated to ask no more, for anyone who should say more would only lie, and the lie would be without profit, for the truth could not be told. Something of it was to be shown in the mystical chastity and the single wholeness of Galahad.

The poem now says that it would be proper to tell of the adventures of the companies, but that shall not yet be, for another branch is to be followed first. This is to be the tale of Merlin.

That last figure of sacred magic, of magic before magic even in art became impermissible, lay to his hand,[1] and he found it—fortunate, and we also. Merlin in this was to be a prophet of the Grail. It was a moment of high poetic alteration. De Borron added here another ancient book to those many of which we have heard in these poems. For he pretended that the hermit to whom Merlin's mother had gone in her distress—he perhaps of whom Layamon had written—was entreated by Merlin to write down the history of these things, and this at first he hesitated to do lest it should lead to sin, but reassured by the wizard, he consented. First he wrote the ancient history of the Grail, and then he turned to Merlin's own life. It is said that the Keepers of the Grail were now in North Britain, and that Blaise was there also.

The tale of his birth, of his coming to Uther Pendragon and of the birth of Arthur, has been given. A great theology was entering the myth. The story of the Round Table was already in existence, but de Borron, if he knew of it, would have nothing of so ordinary a convenience merely for civil peace. The First Table (Merlin said) had been established by Christ himself; the Second by Joseph of Arimathea, at the bidding of Christ himself; the Third was to be by Uther, at the bidding of Merlin. This alteration gives the myth a new stress, for the idea of a spiritual relationship is immediately present, circles of sanctity. The Apostolic company is the first institution; the company of true believers the second; the third is the chivalry of the Table. At the first is our Lord; at the second the fish caught by Bron which was the image of our Lord in the imagination of the young Church,[2] and also the covered vessel of the arch-natural Body and Blood; at the third there is yet nothing, but something is to be. Logres and the Grail are to come together, and the king is to preside at the union. The empty chair—the Siege Perilous

---

[1] Sc. de Borron's. [C. S. L.]

[2] Ἰχθύς (*fish*) was so used because the initial letters of Ἰησοῦς Χριστὸς Θεοῦ Υἱὸς Σωτήρ (*Iesus CHristos THeou Uios Soter*—Jesus Christ, Son of God, Saviour) make up Ἰχθύς (*ichthus*). [C. S. L.]

—is to be left there also till he who was to be the union should come. He was to sit, as it were, in the seat of Judas—and of Moyses—so making up the number of the elect. The Table is to be set up by Uther at Cardoil in Wales, but it is Caerleon which presently seems to stand for the city of Arthur on those far frontiers, near (as it must seem to be) to Broceliande and all that the myth should show living in Carbonek.

There is, however, another poem called *Perlesvaux*, which some suppose to be an early and some a late text. It was translated into English in the nineteenth century by Sebastian Evans. He was a poet of a certain power, though his medievalism is of the usual mannered and slightly picturesque kind common to that period ; if not pre-Raphaelite it is at least kindred to that manner. But this matters less perhaps in a poem of this kind than it might in some medieval texts. And even Wardour Street (though I do not think that Sebastian Evans lived in or anywhere near Wardour Street) is a less falsifying street to read in than—as one might say—certain Athenaeums of the mind. A distinguished modern scholar, writing of Perceval's association with some young woman in a castle, speaks of his ' asceticism ' in not going to bed with her. ' Asceticism ' is a grand word to use for a mere refusal of fornication. Another modern writer says : ' There is more practical moral teaching in Chrétien's Percival than in all the Galahad romances put together.' If this were true—which I do not believe—it would be because the Galahad romances had a greater and more inclusive imagination, and took the moral teaching largely for granted. The figure of the High Prince is for something much more than morals. The Victorians, in spite of the morality attributed to them, did not make these particular mistakes. Tennyson's figure of Galahad is highly inadequate, but its inadequacy is relevant to the original whereas many of the commentators' remarks are not.

The *High History* is the fullest Perceval romance. It does not entirely unite the Arthur theme and the Grail theme, and this is the more disappointing because it starts off as if it were going to do precisely that ; in fact, the opening is very fine and worthy of a greater supernatural story than the *High History*. It is almost the only, if not indeed the only, romance in which the king is himself involved in the visions. Arthur had grown slothful in majesty, to the loss of his reputation and to the distress of Queen Guinevere. This seems, in some sense, to correspond with the unasked question, the lethargy of King Arthur and the languishment of King Fisherman (as he is called here) being of the same kind but in different orders. When King Arthur, to begin to recover his fame, rode out alone on adventure he came to a hermitage where was the dead body of the hermit, and there he heard the voice of Our Lady rebuking the devils and gathering to her the soul of the dead man. In the chapel of another hermitage into which he was not permitted to enter, he saw something of the mystery of the Eucharist. First he saw a very fair woman sitting by the altar with a child on her knee. She gave the child into the hands of the hermit, but when he ' began his sacrament ' the king saw that he held not a child but a man bleeding and thorn-crowned. King Arthur ' seeth him in his own figure . . . and hath pity of him in his heart that he hath seen, and the tears come into his eyes '. A bright light shines ; presently the man is changed again to the child ; and finally at the voice of an angel crying : ' *Ite : missa est* ', the Son and his Mother vanish from the chapel, with ' the fairest company that might ever be seen ', and the light ceases. Afterwards he is told of King Fisherman, the Grail, and the unasked question, and how for want of the question ' all the lands are commoved to war '. Human brotherhood, in fact, has been broken. This is a suggestion of wider scope than the ruin or sterility of the land directly associated with the Castle contains, but it is not further worked out. The king was told also of the Good Knight Perlesvaux, of how his widow mother has been attacked by the Lord of the Moors, and how search is being made for Perlesvaux, or Percival, since only he can aid his mother and heal the distresses of the lands. After hearing of these things, King Arthur returns to Cardoil where he promises Guinevere that he will obey our Saviour's will ; ' " for never had none better desire of well-doing than have I at this time, nor of honour nor of largesse." " Sir," saith she, " God be praised thereof." '

With the exception of the actual coming of Galahad to the court of Arthur in Malory, and the appearance of the veiled Cup, this is the nearest in any of the tales that the king himself comes to the mystery. But in neither this version nor in Malory is he taken farther into it. It is the more disappointing here because he has been allowed to ride out on adventure, and because his own better-doing is intimately connected with both the Eucharist and with King Fisherman. One cannot perhaps say that his interest in the mystery flags, but certainly it seems as if the author is only spasmodically concerned to maintain that interest. The book in fact follows two themes—the Grail theme and the Court theme—and the relation between them is not very close. Other inventions were necessary for that.

Some things, however, are common to both, and of these the most important is the conflict everywhere between ' the old law ' and ' the new law '. The first is paganism ; the second, Christianity. But it is the other phrases which are habitually used ; and the expression of ' the new law ' is in the images of our Lord and his Mother and the Hallows. Its centre, in this story, is the Castle of the Hallows which is also called Eden, the Castle of Joy, and the Castle of Souls. But there is also an indication that this is not the final state ; it is, in its own way, the opening and not the conclusion of the true spiritual knowledge. In the end Perceval himself leaves it and goes to a hermitage in the forest, and the Grail accompanies him.

Perceval is throughout the champion and great master for whose adequate coming everything waits, and this though he himself has been first responsible for the unasked question. He was the son of Alain le Gros—of the lineage of Joseph of Abarimacie—the lord of the Valleys of Camelot. But this Camelot is not King Arthur's ; it ' stood upon the uttermost headland of the wildest isle of Wales by the sea to the West. Nought was there save the hold and the forest and the waters that were round about it. The other Camelot, that was King Arthur's, was situate at the entrance of the kingdom of Logres, and was peopled of folk and was seated at the head of the King's land, for that he had in his governance all the lands that on that side marched with his own.' One cannot say more of this duplication of the name than that it is a duplication and a contrast. One must not symbolically identify them. But at least one may admit that, in reading, an echo passes from one to the other ; and the well-populated city of the king remotely opens upon the solitary hold of the Widow Lady on the uttermost headland of the wildest isle with only the forest and the waters about it. She had three brothers : King Fisherman who kept the Grail in the Castle of Souls ; King Pelles, who had left his crown and become one of the hermits of whom the high strange forest is full ; and the King of Castle Mortal, who has turned to evil, robbed his sister of her inheritance, and is determined to seize on the Grail Castle itself—which indeed, after the death of King Fisherman, he does. It is in the forest that lies, as it were, between the two Camelots that most of the adventures pass. The hermitages are there, with their wise and holy dwellers, ' youthful of seeming, because they serve King Fisherman, and the sweetness of that service is so great that a year seems but a month '. Pageants of mysterious damsels go about it ; and knights of one law or of the other ; and the coming out of it is towards one Camelot or the other, though Perceval and Gawaine and Lancelot and the king ride through it and know both ends.

Gawaine indeed is in this version allowed more than he is given elsewhere. After the opening adventures, the king in the pursuit of well-doing holds ' a high-plenary court ' ; this, in such a romance, is the business of honour and largesse. Gawaine is there engaged to go to King Fisherman ; but when he does so —finding the castle full of chapels, priests, and ancient knights, and in the chief chapel ' the service of the most holy Grail '—he is told by the king that he cannot hope to enter until he brings with him the sword with which St. John Baptist was beheaded, now in the possession of a pagan king. The possession of this he eventually achieves, and brings it to the Fisherman. He is warned again to remember to ask the question. The pageant appears ; one damsel carries the Grail and another the Lance, the point of which bleeds into the Grail. Gawaine ' is thoughtful, and so great a joy cometh to him that naught remembereth he in his thinking save God only '. He seems to see three damsels where he had seen but two and in the midst of the Grail the figure of a child ; afterwards, still among the seeming three damsels, he sees ' the Grail all in flesh, and he seeth above, as him thinketh, a King crowned, nailed upon a rood, and the spear was still fast in his side. Messire Gawaine seeth it and hath great pity thereof, and of nought doth he remember him save of the pain that this King suffereth.' He therefore fails to ask the question, for when the knights and the Master of the knights look and call to him, he remains unconscious of them. ' For the first and only time recorded of him in all the literature, the thought of God overflows his whole consciousness.' [1] He is therefore on the next day compelled to leave the castle, and the dolours remain unhealed.

The achievement of Perceval is a much longer business and has unusual variations. The death of King Fisherman and the seizure of the castle by the King of Castle Mortal are among these. No particular significance in this seems to be suggested ; the Grail and the Hallows withdraw at the moment of the conquest and do not manifest again till Perceval comes. He is much more spiritually related to his mother the Widow Lady and his sister Dindrane, and they to the mysteries. Dindrane's own adventure in the Graveyard . . . [2]

What then is the Achievement of the Grail ? Dante, in a later century, was to put the height of human beatitude in the

---

[1] A. E. Waite : *The Hidden Church of the Holy Grail.*

[2] The sentence is incomplete. In my opinion all that follows probably made part of a separate chapter and there is probably a long hiatus. Others, at least as well qualified as I to judge, think differently. [C. S. L.]

understanding of the Incarnation ; in a lesser, but related, method Angela of Foligno was to speak of knowing ' how God comes into the Sacrament'. To know these things is to be native to them ; to live in the world where the Incarnation and the Sacrament (single or multiple) happen. It is more : it is, in some sense, to live beyond them, or rather (since that might sound profane) to be conscious of them as one is conscious of oneself, Christ-conscious instead of self-conscious. The achievement of the Grail is the perfect fulfilment of this, the thing happening.

It is to the French poets and romancers that we owe the bringing of this high myth into relation with Arthur, King of Britain or Logres ; as it is to Geoffrey of Monmouth that we owe the development of the figure of Arthur the king out of the doubtful records of the Captain-General of Britain ; and as we owe to Sir Thomas Malory the most complete version of the whole in the English language. Much was modified and much added by others. It is perhaps worth while to reshape the whole tale here once more.[1] But we cannot go back behind the royalty which Geoffrey invented. No one can ever uncrown Arthur. The king may have—and indeed must have—the qualities of the Captain-General, but he must be the king.

At a time then when the Roman and Christian civilization in Britain was seriously endangered by the invasions of the pirate and pagan forces, there arose a patriotic movement of considerable force. It was at first led by Aurelius Ambrosius, of a noble Romano-British family ; after his death, his brother Uther, called Pendragon, succeeded to the leadership and by his victories was named for a brief period king of all Britain. He was the father—canonically, but with some strangeness about the birth—of a son, Arthur. At that time the centre of the Roman *imperium* lay in Byzantium. The Empire was Christian, and not only Christian but orthodox and Trinitarian. The Arian heresies had

---

[1] Here the history of the earlier legends ends. What follows describes the growth of the legend in Charles Williams's own mind into the form it has in his poems and was to have in his unwritten poems. [C. S. L.]

been defeated. Christ was adored as God and not as a created being. The variations of this which were called Nestorianism had also been overcome.[1] It had been determined that the mystery of redemption lay not only in the operation of true God but by that operation in flesh and blood. It was generally accepted, though not yet defined, that the Incarnacy deigned to maintain Himself (in His Passion and Resurrection) in His Eucharists. The Pope was in possession of Rome ; about both his figure and that of the remote Emperor in Byzantium there lay something of a supernatural light—at best mystical, at worst magical. There was, for all disputes between East and West, as yet no great schism in Christendom. The prince Arthur grew to youth in that Catholic world ; and this is, eastward from Logres, the condition of his life and reign. But as this is the historic relation, so on the other—westward from Logres—there is the mythical. In a sense, of course, history is itself a myth ; to the imaginative, engaged in considering these things, all is equally myth. We may issue from it into other judgements— doctrinal, moral, historic. But so doing we enter into another kind of thought and judge by other tests—more important perhaps, but not the same. In the myth we need ask for nothing but interior consistency ; thus, if we choose to have it so, there is no reason why Julius Caesar should not hear the souls of the dead putting off in spectral boats from the shores of Gaul. There is no reason why Camus and St. Peter should not both lament Lycidas (for whom, after all, rather than Edward King, Milton supposed himself to be sorrowing. But Edward King *is* Lycidas ? it is certain that Lycidas is something more than Edward King). It is in an ocean where such tales are relevant that Britain lies ; that is why it is Logres, which is Britain in an enlarging world— Britain and more than Britain. It is more like that mysterious Albion of which Blake wrote in another geography.

There lie then near Logres—and they must lie to the west, for to the east we come into history and doctrine and Europe—

---

[1] It is possible that Charles Williams intended to mention more than one heresy, but the text, as it stands, can be defended. [C. S. L.]

other places of the myth. There is the mysterious forest of Broceliande : there are the seas on which the ship of Solomon is to sail ; beyond them is Sarras. It is certainly true that Sarras was originally on the borders of Egypt, but that cannot now be helped, for the lords of the Quest must go there in a ship, and it must lie beyond Carbonek. To send the ship back from Carbonek through the Mediterranean to Egypt—I will not say it could not be done, for anything can be done that can be done, but it seems less convenient than to remove Sarras ; especially as Sarras can be spiritually reached anywhere, but it is not quite suitable that the High Prince should return to the world. He who does that is Bors.

Carbonek itself must be, if not in, at least on the borders of Broceliande. It is the castle of the Hallows ; there are in its chapel the Grail and the Spear. The Spear is that which pierced the heart of Christ ; the Grail is the vessel used at the Last Supper, in which also the blood from the wounded heart was caught. The Keeper of the Castle is the King Pelles, and in the processions of the Grail it is carried by his daughter Helayne. She is maiden, and all but vowed to maidenhood ; only there lies over her the rejection of that desired life ; she is to be the mother of the Grail-lord. It would be perhaps a pity to lose from the tale the other name of Castle Mortal and its king ; but if it is to be kept, there is only one figure who can occupy it, and that is the brother of Pelles, the invisible knight, who is called Garlon. That castle too must stand in Broceliande.

It is indeed in that forest, inextricably mingled with the mystical sea spiritual distance,[1] that all these places of marvel must lie. It is, after all, one of the great forests of myth—greater because of its hidden mysteries than Arden or Birnam or Westermain. The wood of Comus may be compared with it ; and indeed is poetically a part of it, except that it is a holy place and uninhabited by such sorcerers. But some of the outlying parts might be given up to him—until the Judgement. A nobler comparison is with that forest which Dante found at the

---

[1] 'Sea spiritual' (or 'sea-spiritual') is, I think an adjective. [C. S. L.]

foot of the Mount of Purgatory and where he came again to himself, or that other on the height of the Mount where Beatrice came again to him. But it is not proper to do more than shyly observe comparisons between such myths. It is a place of making and of all the figures concerned with making.

Of these one of the most mysterious is Nimue, the Lady of the Lake. Swinburne's great description of her is too effective to be lost. Tennyson turned her into a kind of allegory of the Church, and (if baptism were involved) this might be well enough. But of the two Swinburne's is the greater, for the ecclesiastical and religious figures are already patterned, and the High Prince himself has his own Way, not to be confused. So that Nimue is the great mother and lady of Broceliande—Nature, as it were, or all the vast processes of the universe imaged in a single figure.

There is, however, a problem about Merlin. He is so very much a preparation for the Grail that his earlier diabolic birth seems almost improper to so high a vocation, though it might be worked in well enough. On the other hand there is something attractive in a small invention which would be inconsistent with this diabolic conception. The central fact of the conception of Galahad depends partly on the strange drink given to Lancelot by Brisen, the nurse of Helayne. She in fact prepares within Carbonek what Merlin prophesies and prepares (by his calling of Arthur) in Logres. It might be permissible to make them twins, children of some high parthenogenetical birth of Nimue in Broceliande. They would come then almost like Time and Place to their mission, to prepare in Carbonek and Camelot for the moment of the work.

The calling of Arthur, and the freeing of Logres (or Britain) from the pagans and tyrants is the first movement of the mystery. The Matter of Britain begins with this, leading to the coronation of the king ; when, in the old phrase, ' he put on his crown '. What, however, obviously ought not to happen, and what in Malory and Tennyson is already an almost minor episode, is his war against the Emperor. This was very well in the chivalric battles of Geoffrey, though Nationalism (too often attributed only to the Renascence) is already there getting slightly out of hand. But a kind of supreme wordly glory is Arthur's climax. Even then—by accident or design—he was never allowed to meet the Emperor in battle, and all that Tennyson says is that ' Arthur strove with Rome '. It had better be dropped. No national myth was ever the better for being set against a more universal authority—in our own day we have learnt that—though it might be desirable to heighten the *imperium* in order conveniently to include this royalty within it. But in a myth Byzantium may be many things. It may also be urged, for what the point is worth, that it was in fact this Roman and universal authority for which, in however shadowy a way, the historic Arthur was fighting against the barbarians ; it is not for him himself to fight against it. Nor, now, to win conquests over other nations as such. He is a champion, not a conquistador.

It is in fact here that the centre of the myth must be determined. The problem is simple—is the king to be there for the sake of the Grail or not ? It was so the Middle Ages left it ; but since then it has been taken the other way. The Grail has been an episode. This may still be so, but it can no longer be accidentally so. Tennyson, in that sense, was right ; he meant to make the Grail an episode, and he did. He said it was only for certain people, and he modified the legend accordingly. If it is to be more, it must take the central place. Logres then must be meant for the Grail. (There is a difficulty here about the Dolorous Blow which may be mentioned in a moment.) This indeed must be the pure glory of Arthur and Logres. Vessels of plenty have nothing to do with it ; were it true (as it is not) that the Grail had developed from them, it would still have developed out of all common measurement. It is the central matter of the Matter of Britain. We may, if we choose, reasonably and properly refuse it, but we can hardly doubt that if we do we shall have no doubt a consistent, but a much smaller myth.

For the Grail, so understood, must itself be—I will not say enlarged, for that is impossible, but it must be understood in all its meanings and relationships. It is the tale of Galahad ; it is the tale of the mystical way ; but also it is the tale of the universal way. It is not, as in Tennyson, only for the elect ; it is for all. It is in this sense that the three lords of the Quest are of importance. Bors is in the chapel at Sarras as well as Galahad and Percivale. This is what relates the Achievement to every man. The tale must end, and that part of it when the holy thing returns again to earth—when Galahad is effectually in Bors as Bors is implicitly in Galahad—cannot be told until the clause of the Lord's prayer is fulfilled and the kingdom of heaven is come upon earth, perhaps not until there is a new heaven and a new earth. It must therefore vanish : and Bors must return —in spite of the fact that there are hints, even in Malory, that the mere passage of the Grail destroyed the kingdom. Since the *Grand St. Graal* nothing has ever been quite the same. That romance worked on the literature the effect which the Grail worked on Logres. The only question is whether that work is a necessary part of the Achievement.

If then the Grail is to be fully accepted, in every sense, it must be accepted from the beginning. I have sometimes thought that the best way would be to imagine that Logres was designed to be a place for the coming of the Grail. The immediate expectation of the Second Coming had faded, but the vision of it remained as it has always remained in the Church. It might be taken that the King Pelles, the Keeper of the Hallows, was at the proper time, when Merlin had brought Arthur into his royalty and Logres had been cleared and established, to emerge from Carbonek into Logres, directing the processions of the Grail and the prelude of the Second Coming. Logres was to be blessed thus, and he who said Mass in Sarras would say it in Caerleon and Camelot as he did in Jerusalem. This, however, is but one means to making the tale coherent, and need not be pressed. The more urgent problems are the place of the unasked question and of the Dolorous Blow. They are, of course, strictly speaking, alternatives. It is certain that we must keep the Dolorous Blow ; a loss of that would mean a loss of the Wounded King, which cannot be imagined. The only question is whether we can have the unasked question also.

It would not be impossible, if the whole thing were regarded as a tale of the Fall—individual or universal. The union would be in the fact that the lack of the question would mean the lack of an answer, and hence an ignorance of the true nature of the Invisible Knight. This was one of the secrets Gawaine should have learned and reported ; not learning and not reporting, he left the Court ignorant and Balin the Savage free to avenge his host's son. The refusal to ask the question is precisely that refusal to inquire which accompanies so many a temptation and encourages so many a sin. ' What serves the Grail ? ' The answer is ' You and all Logres '. It is not so much the encouragement of a sin that is so often sinful as a refusal to encourage the counter-movement, the opposite of a sin. After that, the ignorant savage is free.

The Dolorous Blow consisted in the wounding of the royal Keeper of the Hallows with the Sacred Spear. The Spear was that which had wounded the side of Christ, and it bled continually at the point. It was then aimed at the central heart. But when Balin le Sauvage used it, he used it for his own self-preservation. It is this turning of the most sacred mysteries to the immediate security of the self that is the catastrophic thing. It is indeed, morally, precisely the wounding of the Keeper of the Hallows which then takes place. Man wounds himself. It is an image of the Fall ; it is also an image of every individual and deliberate act of malice, though the deliberation is here but passionate and not coldly angry.

It has, of course, every excuse. The mystery of the Invisible Knight—say, the Invisible Slayer—is abroad in the world. He might have been explained, had the question been asked. As it is, he rides destructively, but in the hall of Carbonek he is at last seen and known ; it may be that even there he was a dark knight, and perhaps the King or Duke of Castle Mortal, since one must not over-multiply the title of king. There is here a certain similitude to the figure of the Holy Ghost, as It exercises Its operations in the world. For Balin actually to kill an inhabitant of Broceliande can hardly be allowed : the forest and its people are not of a kind that could be overcome in that manner. But the ever-bleeding wound of the Keeper is exactly symbolical, and so is the ruin that falls on Logres. A new darkness and sterility begin to creep through the land from which the pagans have been expelled. The outer conquests are not the inner. Victory is being still celebrated in Camelot when defeat issues from Carbonek.

This, even in the direct incidents of the tale, is not an exaggeration. One incident is directly the consequence of the Dolorous Blow ; and there is another like it which should be. The first is that Balin the Savage in ignorance kills his own brother Balan, and Balan him. The natural pieties begin to be lost, and there is incivility in the blood. It is in fact the farther externalization of the Wounded King. But the disorder spreads farther. In the first tales Mordred was the king's nephew ; in later versions he became the king's son by incest, but unknown incest. The queen Morgause of Orkney, the wife of King Lot, was Arthur's sister. But he does not know this when she comes to his court, and he tempts her to lie with him. The birth of that incestuous union is Mordred, and the fate of the Round Table comes into the world almost before the Table has been established ; say, at the very feast of the crowning of Arthur and the founding of the Table. The seed of its destroyer lies in the womb of Morgause while she watches the ceremonies. This is not irony ; it is something beyond irony. No doubt the wise young master Merlin knows, but it is not for him to speak, or only in riddles. He knows that the egress of the Grail from Carbonek has now been prevented, but also he prepares the Perilous Seat. He sets that empty chair among all the chairs ; he promises an achievement, and a restoration from a destruction which is known then to him alone.

This now is the double way of Logres, of the Table, and of

the king. The glory of Arthur continues. He marries Guinevere—the most beautiful woman. He has for friend and chief lord Lancelot, the bravest and noblest man. Lancelot is chief in the heart of both the king and the queen. It was a wise instinct that kept the old writers from making Arthur himself a lord in love between a man and a woman. It is the high brotherhood of arms and friendship in which he is noble ; that is his own personal share in the glory of his kingdom. But it is an actual kingdom and an actual glory : that is, Lancelot has his proper duties to the State. The political side of the kingdom is not to be denied or despised, and the Table itself is a part of the settlement. All the champions are still to be champions of the good ; in that Tennyson was right, though he perhaps a little slurred the inevitable dullness of their duty. The Table is a gathering of the realm as well as of knighthood, and if Lancelot is not a Chancellor or Prime Minister he is not unlike. It is observable that in the great parting with Guinevere in Malory he tells her that he would have achieved the Grail ' had not your lord been '. This may refer to the love-conflict, but then one would have expected ' had not you been '. It may again be an error, [1] but if it is not, then it is important. For then we have a definite relation of Lancelot to a more complete way of the Affirmation of Images than has been allowed to him. It is not only to do with a woman, but with men and women ; not only with the queen but with the Republic.

The speech of Sir Ector over the dead Lancelot confirms this. Lancelot, for all the errands upon which he rides, is never merely a knight-errant. He affirms friendship, courtesy, justice, and nobility—in all the references allowed them. He is almost the active centre of that kingdom of which Arthur is, in a sense, the passive. Arthur, of course, is no such poor thing, but it is true he does not *seem* to act.

Lancelot then is the chief figure of the Way of Affirmations.

---

[1] It almost certainly is. Malory XXI. ix reads *lord*, but Winchester MS. (ed. F. Vinaver, Oxford, 1947, Vol. III, p. 1253) reads *love*. The Winchester text was, of course, inaccessible when Charles Williams wrote. [C. S. L.].

The great Arthuriad is no longer a division between this and its opposite and complementary companion—the Way of Rejections. The tales of Arthur and of the Grail, of Camelot and Carbonek, may have been as antagonistic in their first invention as scholars maintain. They are now no longer so. There is, no doubt, a separation, but the separation is the union ; and this is not so alien from our experience that we need reject in myth what we have to accept in mere living. The moral of the whole is as firm as ever Tennyson would have made it, but it is deeper in its metaphysic.

Between Guinevere and Lancelot there has risen this fatal love—fatal but not fated. No magical potion has been its source, such as Tristram and Iseult drank between sea and sky. The spring, and young blood, and generous hearts, are its beginning. Guinevere has always been a slight difficulty, for in the situation of the tale, she has nothing to do but to be in love with Lancelot. He can ride out, and have adventures, and return, but she can only sit and work at embroideries and love. It is therefore only in relation to that that she has hitherto existed. I suppose something more might be done with her ; her royalty might be stressed in actions. But it has not yet happened. Her phrases are love's phrases—embittered or noble. ' And so I report me unto all the Table Round ', etc. She retains to the end that capacity for stabbing at Lancelot ; it is to be forgiven because of her very great dolour, and because it is not for us to revenge what Lancelot accepted.

I am not sure that, for all Chrétien de Troyes and the others did with it, the great love-tale comes properly now under the heading of Romantic Love, either in the historic or the metaphysical sense. It began certainly with Romance. But Malory, as was said, has made it different. It is the affirmation of one kind of image and not of another. It is certainly not any nonsense of the ' death-wish ' as M. de Rougemont suggests. Malory knows nothing of lovers who desire to perish. Subconsciously ? Nor that ; through all their beings these great lovers desire life, honour, and reciprocal joy. Some such element might—though

I do not much believe it—be felt in the Tristram drink, though in Malory Tristram shows little enough awareness of it. But Lancelot and the queen are simply not of that kind at all. Any more than we are—in spite of our occasional dark indulgence of ourselves in our sorrows.

It is indeed their situation—in life and desire for life—which in Malory offers such profound hints. The soul, affirming the validity of those images which appear to it, finds itself, physically or mentally, caught in its own desire to appropriate them. The temptation of the king—were it stressed, but it is not— would be to be too much himself the State ; to appropriate Logres to himself. The temptation of Lancelot is to appropriate the queen. It is no less a temptation of the soul that it appears as a temptation of the body. It is a temptation of power. Power is not something that one has ; it is something one is. The desire for power is always being thwarted by this misunderstanding. One is not powerful. But if one had x one would be powerful. Power (as Wordsworth showed us) is in one's capacities. The capacities of Lancelot and the queen are distracted.

It is, however, by indirect means that these two great Powers are fulfilled. One must learn to think properly of the personages of the myth, and not less mightily than the names deserve. The Arthuriad recedes into dim forests and seas, and the ship of Solomon driving into the last Mysteries, and in the foreground is a Saracen knight hunting a strange beast which is known by the sound of barking dogs. It is called the Blatant Beast, and when Spenser took it over he turned it into the mob, but it is not that in Malory ; it is only a figure of fable, except that its Paynim pursuer will not be christened till he has overcome it. But he has another quality too, which is his hopeless love for the queen Iseult, but it was Tristram whom she loved and she took no care for Palomides. (And a distinction between ways of thought is between Malory and Austin Dobson's short poem.) These two might well, in some way, be one ; and it is perhaps significant that Palomides is at last christened after his reconciliation with

Tristram (but not with Mark—but of Mark we need say nothing), and that nothing in the end is heard of any seizing of the Blatant Beast.

There is, however, another point where Palomides comes violently into the myth. It is at the famous—and oddly named —Tournament of Lonazep. It is there that Palomides does his greatest deeds—' it is his day ', said Sir Dinadan—but also his worst ; for he overthrows Lancelot by falsehood.

WILLIAMS AND THE ARTHURIAD
by C. S. Lewis

Preliminary

Here the Fragment ends, and there is no certain evidence how the book would have gone on. In the papers entrusted to me I find the following List of Contents : 1. *The Origin of the Figure.* 2. *The Celtic Tales.* 3. *Geoffrey of Monmouth.* 4. *The Great Inventions.* 5. *The Tudor Revival.* 6. *Malory.* 7. *Spenser.* 8. *The Augustans and Romantics.* 9. *The Victorians.* 10. *The Matter of Britain.* 11. *Galahad.* It will be seen that the earlier chapters in this list do not correspond exactly with the chapters actually written and it is even possible that some of the material which might originally have been intended for the two last (and mysteriously named) chapters has actually been embodied in the last pages of the fragment. We have also a single page (entitled *The Figure of Arthur*) which appears to be a preface, or, in view of its brevity, a 'prefatory note'. It reads as follows :—

The Figure of Arthur

This book is a consideration of the tale of King Arthur in English literature. It does not pretend to investigate, or indeed to record, the original sources, the Celtic tales or the French romances, except in so far as some mention of them is necessary to the main theme. That theme is the coming of two myths, the myth of Arthur and the myth of the Grail ; of their union ; and of the development of that union not only in narrative complexity but in intellectual significance. The book begins with the earliest appearances of both and traces them to the great English presentation in Malory. Malory, however, as we at present have him, never quite fulfilled the hints of profound meaning which are scattered through him. After Malory the political effort of Henry VII to derive his dynasty from Arthur distracted attention from the Grail, and there came the modified Arthur of Spenser. It was not until the nineteenth century that both the king and the Grail began seriously to return, and the great Victorians are shown as labouring to re-express a text their ancestors had defaced. Even they, however, tended (as in general we do to-day) to regard the Lancelot-Guinevere story as more important than that of the Grail ; or if not, certainly to regard them as in conflict. In one sense, this must inevitably be so ; but in another it is not so at all. The great invention of Galahad is as much of a union and a redemption as of a division and a destruction. It is his double office with which the book is concerned, and the final chapter discusses the developed significance of the whole myth.

In this, it is worth noticing, the 'Tudor Revival' which came, oddly, before Malory in the List of Contents is placed after him. The List of Contents, in fact, disagrees with the Prefatory Note, with the Fragment as actually written, and with chronology, and has no value as evidence of what Williams was really going to do. I take it to be no more than a product of that day-dreaming with a pen in the hand which is often the first step towards writing a book. Williams would not have been ill-pleased at our drawing a parallel from what appear to have been Milton's methods of composition. In the Trinity MS. we find four drafts for a tragedy on the Fall of Man. The only lines we now have which are known with certainty (many are suspected) to have been part of that tragedy are the opening of Satan's address to the Sun in the fourth book of *Paradise Lost*. Our informant, Milton's nephew, tells us they were to have been the beginning of the tragedy. But none of the drafts begins with a speech by Satan. No doubt Milton's nephew may have made a mistake ; but it seems to me just as likely that Milton dreamed with pen in hand, that the drafts were mirages which vanished when real composition began.

The only contribution I can make towards filling up the gap left by the end of the fragment is a very meagre one and consists of two remarks which I heard Williams make about Tennyson's *Idylls of the King*. One was on *Merlin and Vivien* where he thought the story of Sir Sagramore's nocturnal misadventure altogether too domestic and modern—' too like Pickwick ', he said.   On the other hand he praised the lines about Launcelot, which some quote with derision,

> His honour rooted in dishonour stood
> And faith unfaithful kept him falsely true,

as a very concise and accurate description of the situation in which innumerable human beings have found themselves.

In the last pages of the Fragment we have already been allowed to see the Arthurian story re-shaping itself in Williams's mind. There is no question here of a modern artist approaching the old material as a quarry from which he can chip what he pleases, responsible only to his own modern art.   It is more a ' dove-like brooding ', a watching and waiting as if he watched a living thing, now and then putting out a cautious finger to disentangle two tendrils or to train one a little further towards the support which it had already almost reached, but for the most part simply waiting.   Nominally he is writing criticism or literary history, but in reality creation is going on.   Perhaps if he had not been nominally writing criticism he could not have given us so deep an insight into the process whereby his own Arthuriad came into existence.

To that poem I now invite the reader to turn.   The thirty-two lyrical pieces of which it consists are distributed between two volumes, twenty-four in *Taliessin through Logres* and eight in *The Region of the Summer Stars*.   In the chronology of Williams's literary career probably all (and certainly some) of those in *The Region* are later than any in *Taliessin* ; but in the chronology or Arthurian Britain they are not systematically arranged.   I do not know whether he would so have arranged them if he had lived to complete the cycle, but a mere commentator must get the imaginary chronology clear.   I deal with them in what I take to be their chronological order, omitting the two *Preludes* which naturally stand outside the time-scheme and which will be readily understood when the cycle has been mastered as a whole. The backward and forward links by which I establish the position of each poem will (I hope) become clear in the course of the

exposition. Sometimes I am in doubt ; and I hope that the
fame of the poem will not grow so slowly but that before I die
I may see 'Williams scholarship' sweeping my whole chronology
away and allotting me my place among the pre-scientific primi-
tives. For the moment, however, I am taking the poems, and
advising the beginner to take them, in the following order.

From *The Region* : The Calling of Taliessin.
  From *Taliessin* : The Calling of Arthur.
               The Vision of the Empire.
               Taliessin's Return to Logres.
               Mount Badon.
               The Crowning of Arthur.
               Taliessin's Song of the Unicorn.
               Bors to Elayne : the Fish of Broceliande.
               Taliessin in the School of the Poets.
               Taliessin on the Death of Virgil.
               The Coming of Palomides.
               Lamorack and the Queen Morgause of Orkney.
               Bors to Elayne : on the King's Coins.
               The Star of Percivale.
               The Ascent of the Spear.
               The Sister of Percivale.

From *The Region* : The Founding of the Company.
               Taliessin in the Rose Garden.
               The Departure of Dindrane.
               The Queen's Servant.

  From *Taliessin* : The Son of Lancelot.
               Palomides before his Christening.
               The Coming of Galahad.
               The Departure of Merlin.
               The Death of Palomides.
               Percivale at Carbonek.

From *The Region* : The Meditation of Mordred.
  From *Taliessin* : The Last Voyage.
From *The Region* : The Prayers of the Pope.
  From *Taliessin* : Taliessin at Lancelot's Mass.

The Establishment of Arthur

THE best method of surveying the poem as a whole will be to follow the history of Taliessin himself. He is not, perhaps, the hero as older poets would have understood the word 'hero'; that position belongs more to Galahad. But he is the character through whom the poet (and therefore the readers) most often look at the world. By attaching ourselves to him and dealing with the main regions of Williams's poetic universe one by one as Taliessin comes to them, we shall find a ready-made order for our exposition. Otherwise we should be at a loss where to begin; for many 'huge cloudy symbols' of equal importance, and inter-related with sensitive complexity, demand our attention.

Taliesin—the name means Radiant Brow—is a poet and magician in the *Mabinogion*. Tennyson in the *Idylls of the King* made him the principal poet at the court of Arthur and by slipping an extra *s* into his name (Taliessin) made it a better word for English ears.

The Calling of Taliessin opens with a sort of cloud-landscape of the Welsh legends about Taliessin's birth. The passage can, if you wish, be analysed by a glance at the originals in the *Mabinogion*, but I doubt if this is necessary. The note is one of agnosticism: 'none knew; no clue he showed'. The absolute beginnings of poethood are a mystery. Nothing comes into focus till we see the child with his bright forehead lying at the weir and Elphin's [1] men drawing him to shore. Then, instantly, the focus brightens into hard light : we are assisting at a moment of decision. Elphin and his men can accept or reject this stranger, this gift of the river. The choice, whether they know it or not,

[1] A lineal descendant of this Elphin was among Williams's friends at Oxford during the war years.

will make or unmake in each of them that state of affairs which Williams calls ' the city '. Our reaction to new poetry—to poetry itself—is not an affair of chance : here also we have free will. Elphin is a healthy barbarian. His vocation is of the blood rather than the intelligence and his idea of poetry hardly goes beyond ' a chorus after a meal '. The child is already singing—singing of the strange metamorphoses which led up to its supernatural birth. Elphin understands little of it, but the song conforms to an established ' code '. I think this means that it involves Druidical doctrines of re-incarnation with which Elphin is familiar, for the poetic child is a pagan and the Lord God has not yet ' shown him the doctrine of largesse in the land of the Trinity '. There is possibly a hint here that Karma itself might be not so much an illusion as a part of that ' law ' from which the Redemption has set us free.

The upshot is that Elphin adopts him, and the next paragraph describes his childhood and his riddling answers to those who asked his lineage. These are mainly adapted from the ' Second Answer to Maelgwn ' in the *Mabinogion* but so adapted as to state Williams's own myth of the birth of poetic genius. The passage is thus to be read with a kind of double vision ; with one eye on the Welsh legends about Ceridwen and her cauldron and the other on the cosmic history of the Heavenly Muse—a wonder whose origin is unknown, whose native region is the summer stars, who was a spectator of creation, and has shared (beyond or before time) in the travail of the Redemption. At the close we descend sharply to the poet, the individual human vehicle of the Muse. He is in this world an oddity ; there is something about him too numinous for ordinary human flesh—' therefore no woman will ever wish to bed me '. This will become important later in the poem. According to Williams the poet is not, except by accident or in some peculiar mode, a lover, or at least, not a successful lover ; he is the cause of love between others, the Hymen to nuptials he does not himself enjoy.

Growing thus among the Welsh tribes the young Taliessin hears rumours of ' the Empire '. While they are only rumours it may suffice us to say that the Empire is Byzantium. And, hearing of the Empire, he hears also of Christianity—of the Fall and of the Incarnation. ' Dim and far ' though these rumours may be, they are enough to make pagan poetry and pagan magic seem poor and ' goetic '. (*Magia* and *goetia*, as used by Renaissance occultists, mean ' white ' and ' black ' magic respectively.) In pursuit of the Empire, Byzantium, ' the city ', the boy sets out on his travels.

His course runs somewhere down the West coast of Britain—perhaps along the Severn Sea or further West even to Cornwall. On his left lies what will later be Logres (Arthurian Britain), but Arthur has not yet arisen. Logres is as yet ' without the form of a republic ', it is merely ' a storm of violent kings at war '. But on his right hand—towards the Atlantic and also *in* the Atlantic—lies something more dangerous still, the Wood of Broceliande. His road curves close up to the Wood. Terror besets him. He fears that he may lose his humanity (' fall from his kind ') ; he feels ' universal spirit ' rising wild and savage against his own personal spirit. We must here make our first halt, to contemplate the nature of Broceliande.

A note in my own hand (but it is either transcribed or abridged from a letter of Williams's) runs as follows. ' Broceliande, West of Logres, off Cornwall ; both a forest and a sea—a sea-wood. It joins the sea of the Antipodes. Beyond it (at least beyond a certain part of it) is Carbonek ; then the open sea ; then Sarras. A place of making, home of Nimue. From it the huge shapes emerge, the whole *matter* of the *form* of Byzantium —and all this is felt in the beloved.'

Carbonek is the castle of the holy things, the dwelling place of Pelles the guardian of the Grail. Sarras is the ' land of the Trinity '. If both these are beyond Broceliande or at least *beyond a certain part of it*—then through Broceliande runs the road from earth to heaven. On the other hand Broceliande, if you follow it far enough and in a certain direction, will bring you right round the world to the ' antipodean ocean ' ; and indeed, even from the shore of Britain, Taliessin can discern through

the trees of Broceliande its 'thrusting inlets'.   Now the Antipodean Ocean, in Williams's myth, is the realm of P'o-Lu.
There the Headless Emperor walks forever backwards and
'heaven-sweeping tentacles stretch, dragging octopus bodies
over the level'.   Consciousness in P'o-Lu consists only of
'rudiments or relics', 'the turmoil of the mind of sensation'.
It is on the very fringe of Hell.   For either journey, then, to
Sarras or to P'o-Lu, Broceliande may be the route ; *tenent media
omnia silvae.*

Those who accomplish either journey will not be likely to
return ; but those who have gone only a little way into the wood
have been known to come out again.   They are changed when
they do, and that in one or other of two ways.   Some are 'dumb
and living, like a blest child in a mild and holy sympathy of joy'.
But the majority came back as *cranks*—panacea-mongers 'loqua-
cious with a graph or a gospel, gustily audacious'.

Inside the wood it is very quiet

> there no strife
> is except growth from the roots, nor reaction but repose ;
> vigours of joy drive up ; rich-ringed moments
> thick in their trunks thrive, young-leaved their voices.

For there is no time in Broceliande

> moons and suns that rose in rites and runes
> are come away from sequence, from rules of magic ;
> here all is cause and all effect . . .

> Time's president and precedent, grace ungrieved,
> floating through gold-leaved lime or banked behind beech
> to opaque green, through each membraned and tissued experience
> smites in simultaneity to times variously veined.[1]

In a writer whose philosophy was Pantheistic or whose poetry
was *merely* romantic this formidable wood from whose quiet
and timeless fecundity 'the huge shapes emerge' would undoubtedly figure as the Absolute itself.   And indeed Broceliande
is what most romantics are enamoured of ; into it good mystics

[1] From *The Departure of Merlin.*

and bad mystics go : it is what you find when you step out of
our ordinary mode of consciousness. You find it equally in
whatever direction you step out. All journeys away from the
solid earth are equally, at the outset, journeys into the abyss.
Saint, sorcerer, lunatic, and romantic lover all alike are drawn
to Broceliande, but Carbonek is beyond *a certain part of it* only.
It is by no means the Absolute. It is rather what the Greeks
called the *Apeiron*—the unlimited, the formless origin of forms.
Dante and D. H. Lawrence, Boehme and Hitler, Lady Julian
and the Surrealists, had all been there. It is the home of immense
dangers and immense possibilities.

The sovereign mistress of Broceliande is by Williams named
Nimue—a person who has almost nothing in common with
Malory's Nimue. To say that Nimue is an image of Nature is
true, but not very helpful since ' Nature ' itself is a hard word.
For Williams, as for Plato, the phenomenal world—the world
studied by the sciences—is primarily a reflection or copy or
adaptation of something else. Nimue, the ' mother of making ',
is that energy which reproduces on earth a pattern derived from
' the third heaven ', i.e. from the sphere of Venus, the sphere of
Divine Love. But the poet does not use those words. What
resides in the third heaven (' the pattern in heaven of Nimue,
time's mother on earth ') is called by him ' the feeling intellect '
or *mens sensitiva*. The expression ' feeling intellect ' is borrowed
from Wordsworth's *Prelude* (xiv. 226) and the whole passage in
which it occurs is a comment on the later poet's meaning.
Wordsworth has just emerged into clear moonlight on the top
of Snowdon and there looked down on the sea of mist out of
which ' mounted the roar of waters '. This scene has become
to him a symbol of the human mind in what Wordsworth
believed to be its highest condition ; and the various names
which he uses to indicate that condition (imagination, power,
spiritual love) are all, on Williams's view summed up in l. 226 as
' the height of feeling intellect '. The important difference
between the two poets is that where Wordsworth is thinking of
a subjective state in human minds, Williams is thinking of an

objective celestial fact. The Feeling Intellect may be attained for moments by human beings ; but it exists as a permanent reality in the spiritual world and by response to that archtype Nimue brings the whole process of nature into being. Williams is here (perhaps unconsciously) reproducing the doctrine of the Renaissance Platonists that Venus—celestial love and beauty— was the pattern or model after which God created the material universe. (Hence in *The Faerie Queene*, III. vi. 12, the sphere of Venus is ' The house of goodly formes and faire aspect Whence all the world derives the glorious Features of Beautie ').

But all this time Taliessin waits upon his road in terror under the eaves of the forest. We must return to him.

Here, as he hesitates, he is met by two luminous forms. They are Merlin and Brisen. They have come out of Broceliande because they are the son and daughter of Nimue. They are called respectively ' Time and space, duration and extension ' : all the works of Nimue, except where Grace intervenes, are subject to these two. They call to Taliessin and tell him their present business. They are sent to set up in Logres a kingdom which shall be like the holy kingdom of Pelles at Carbonek. It is to be the kingdom of a complete and balanced humanity, for ' The Empire and Broceliande shall meet in Logres '. It is not yet time to exhibit the nature of the Empire, but this line is our first hint. That man would be complete in whom Byzantium and Broceliande were wholly at one—the wood wholly informed by the city, the city fully energized by the wood.

Taliessin understands little of what they say, but he bivouacs with them for the night and between sleeping and waking sees the sacred incantations with which they begin their task. This movement is ushered in by an image of startling beauty. The Earth's shadow, as we all know, is a cone—a dunce's cap of darkness. The point of that cone is here supposed to touch the sphere of Venus : thus Nimue's agents stand at its base while Nimue's archtype receives its point. Continuity is established between the natural order, the manifold and unstable ectype, and its ' climax tranquil in Venus ' where the ' unriven truths ' dwell—the unities which down here become multiplicities. We are, in fact, watching the impregnation of Nimue by her Pattern (*materia appetit formam ut virum femina*). The active force of the Feeling Intellect becomes audible to Merlin and Brisen as ' a faint, beelike humming'. All that has been produced or will be produced on earth already exists or still exists up at the ' tranquil climax' but differently—

> in the third heaven
> the stones of the waste glimmered like summer stars.

Taliessin, dimly aware of what they are doing, cannot understand it. That is because, though a poet, he is still only a poet, and

> The weight of poetry could not then sink
> into the full depth of the weight of glory.

He is even only a pagan, druidical poet ; and the Druids, as I learn from one of Williams's own notes, represent ' a kind of ancient earthy poetry—say, like Wordsworth'. He has not yet been to Byzantium. Yet he has already a confused premonition of his journey thither. He sees in his dream what I take to be Sarras itself

> a clear city on a sea-site
> in a light that shone from behind the sun,

and the court of Arthur, the Grail, the Grail Ship, and Dindrane, sister of Percivale.

With the morning comes clarity. ' Go to Byzantium' commands Merlin, and adds that the great design of founding Logres may in fact end in failure. He and Brisen have ' prepared the ambiguous rite for either chance'. But if it fails, Taliessin will still have a work to perform : out of the very failure of the main design, if it does fail, a new function will emerge. Taliessin obeys and after bidding farewell to Merlin and Brisen continues his journey to Byzantium. Merlin goes on his great errand to Logres.

In *The Calling of Arthur* this errand is performed. Famine lies

upon the land and 'snow falls over brick and prickle' when
Arthur is met by Merlin crying 'Now am I Camelot : now am
I to be builded'. The eleven kings against whom, in Malory,
Arthur fought to win his throne, are here reduced to one—
Cradlemas, King of London. By a happy and unexpected
invention Cradlemas is made not a barbarian but the last feeble,
fragile, and sinister representative of Roman civilization. He
has (like Nero) an emerald for a monocle and wears a gilded
mask ; his 'high aged voice squeals' with hypocritical and
unhelpful pity for his starving subjects. The lyric ends in a
fierce, glad rush of music as the builders, the food-bringers, the
saviours overwhelm Cradlemas like a tide ;

> Arthur ran ; the people marched : in the snow
>   King Cradlemas died in his litter ; a screaming few
>   fled ; Merlin came ; Camelot grew.
> In Logres the king's friend landed, Lancelot of Gaul.

In the next piece (*The Vision of the Empire*) we find that
Taliessin has arrived at Byzantium. Striking into this 'greater
ode' at the third paragraph we find, indeed, that Taliessin has
already had his audience with the Emperor : we meet him
coming away from it, coming from 'the exposition of grace'
back 'to the place of images'. Before we can understand this
we must study Byzantium at some length.

For the purposes of the poem it is feigned that Arthurian
Britain was a province or 'theme' of the Byzantine empire ;
and it is important to remember that the word ' theme ' wherever
it occurs has its Byzantine sense of ' province '. The whole plan
for the union in Logres of Broceliande and the Empire, the whole
conception of Arthur's kingdom and the offered grace of the
Grail, are attributed to the Emperor. From this point of view
the Emperor symbolizes God. But simply to state this equiva-
ence, and leave it at that, is to kill the living symbolism. We
must see with our imaginations why God should be so envisaged.

The image of the Empire is the final form of something that
had always haunted Williams and which he often referred to

simply as ' the city '. The word is significant. Williams was a Londoner of the Londoners ; Johnson or Chesterton never exulted more than he in their citizenship. On many of us the prevailing impression made by the London streets is one of chaos ; but Williams, looking on the same spectacle, saw chiefly an image—an imperfect, pathetic, heroic, and majestic image— of Order. Two passages from among many in his novels may be quoted. One is from *War in Heaven* (Chapter V) where he is describing the decline of what had once been a residential street. At least, one end of the street shows mere decline. But at the other end new life is beginning for there ' a public house signalized the gathering of another code of decency and morals which might in time transform the intervening decay '. The proletarian courtesy and community of a public house (with all the mutual forbearance and observance of unwritten law which they imply) are a manifestation of ' the city '. The other passage comes from *The Greater Trumps*. It comes from Chapter 4 and the reference to ' the Emperor ' is explained by the fact that Henry and Nancy have just been studying the Tarot cards. They are in a car and have come to a traffic block ;

' A policeman's hand held them up. Henry gestured towards it. " Behold the Emperor ! " he said to Nancy. " You're making fun of me," she half protested. " Never less," he said seriously. " Look at him " . . . She saw in that heavy official barring their way the Emperor of the Trumps, helmed, in a white cloak, stretching out one sceptred arm, as if Charlemagne or one like him stretched out his controlling sword over the tribes of Europe pouring from the forests. . . . The noise of all the pausing street came upon her as the roar of many peoples ; the white cloak held them by a gesture : order and law were there.'

Such is Byzantium—Order, envisaged not as restraint nor even as a convenience but as a beauty and splendour. Perhaps no element in Williams's imagination separates him so widely as this from other writers. The modern world has planners and orderers in plenty, but they are not often poets : it has poets not a few, but they seldom see beauty in policemen.

Yet order, in the sense of discipline and civility, is not the whole of what Williams sees in Byzantium : if it were, the Roman empire might have been as apt an image as the Byzantine. He chooses the Byzantine because, whether rightly or wrongly,[1] we think of it as something more rigid, more stylized, more scrupulously hierarchical, more stiffly patterned than the Roman. Its organization suggests something geometrical ; and that was what Williams desired. His great saying ' Hell is inaccurate ' implies his outlook on heaven. Deeply moved by even human order, he was also deeply aware of Divine Order as something of a flawless and mathematic precision imposing itself on the formless flux of natural moods and passions, imposing itself in the shape of virtue, courtesy, intelligence, ritual. Thus the *Peras* (limit) met the *Apeiron*, the Empire met Broceliande. Thus he complained that the word *glory* in English tended to mean a ' mazy bright blur ' whereas ' the maze should be exact and the brightness should be that of a geometrical pattern ' (*He Came Down from Heaven*, p. 39). Plato and the Hebrew prophets seemed to him to agree in teaching that ' God always geometrizes ' (ibid. p. 40). Sin could be defined as ' the preference of an immediately satisfying experience to the believed pattern of the universe ; one may even say to the pattern of the glory '. Hence his insistence, all through the poems, on precision, accuracy, straightness, definition. St. Paul in the Prelude to the *Region* ' *defines* the physiological glory ' (that is, the Incarnation). Palomides longs for ' the *accurate* flash ' of ' Iseult's eyes '. The young poets at the bardic school in Camelot ' study *precision* ', Merlin ' *defines* the blazons of the brain ', Taliessin speaks of 'the *balance and poise* needful to all joys '. Straight rods, hazel rods, now used for measuring-rods, now for whipping disorderly slaves, now as the ' implacable hazels ' of incantation, are a recurring image.

At this stage we become aware of one aspect in which Taliessin

[1] Fr. Gervase Matthew, O.P., tells me that Williams's picture of Byzantium catches some aspects of the historical reality better than Gibbon's : though Gibbon was at first Williams's only source.

is the symbol of his creator.   He comes out of Wales and legend and old Druidic poetry into the geometric world of Byzantium and only by so doing becomes useful to Logres.   Something of the same sort has happened to romantic poetry itself in the person of Williams ; for he starts from the very depth of the romantic tradition and, without ceasing to be romantic, advances to the acceptance of all that is at first sight furthest from romanticism. In him the poetic tradition which had begun in Pantheism, antinomianism, and revolt, ends in Nicene theology, moral severity, and the celebration of order.   His ideal poetry is that which can ' grow mature with pure fact '.

The throne-room of the Emperor of Byzantium from which we see Taliessin returning here typifies the presence of God: an audience with the Emperor, the vision of God.   It is the central unity : all creation is simply an expression in infinitely varied forms of that one basic reality—' The streets repeat the sound of the Throne '.   In order that we finite beings may apprehend the Emperor He translates His glory into multiple forms—into stars, woods, waters, beasts, and the bodies of men.   His ' household ' and ' logothetes ' ' abate the identities of creation ' for the benefit of ' kinds and kindreds ' ; turn the noumenal unity into a multitude of phenomena.   When Taliessin returns from the throne-room down the porphyry stairs he is coming back to the ' place of images ', as it were, to the created universe which is an image of the uncreated.   If you prefer it, he is turning from the vision of God enjoyed in a moment of devotion to that indirect vision of God which a good man and a good poet enjoys in such ' images ' as poetry, earthly order, and romantic love.   All round him he hears the ' clatter ' of the chariots which are leaving Byzantium in every direction to bear the Divine messages through the world.   But because he is still fresh from the Centre he can see the whole Empire in its true or inner significance.

Thus seen, the Empire reveals itself as an ' organic body ', a human body.   Conversely, the human body, seen in the light of the Throne, is an image of the Empire, of the Kingdom of

107

God. That is the explanation of the end-leaf of *Taliessin through Logres* which may have puzzled some readers.

The second strophe of the Ode describes that ' theme ' of the Empire which William calls Caucasia. As will be seen from the end-leaf, Caucasia in the anatomical myth becomes what Rousseau called *l'objet ridicule* ; what Williams calls ' the rounded bottom of the Emperor's glory ' or ' the lost name, the fool's shame '. Whether ridiculous or not, whether shameful or not, the image is a dominant one throughout the poems. Williams's own note on Elburz may be helpful—' A Caucasian mountain : type of the lowness and height, fertility and chastity, verdure and snow, of the visible body. Also the scene of Prometheus' martyrdom. The bringing of fire for every purpose.' From this it will be seen that Caucasia is not so much a particular part of the body as the whole body, or even the whole man, seen from a particular point of view. Caucasia is natural pleasure, natural beauty, health, physical energy, the whole natural basis of our lives. In fallen Man it is ' the natural man ' or ' old Adam ' ; hence in *The Ascent of the Spear* when the slave sits in the stocks ' the Caucasian theme ' *aches*. This has two meanings : firstly, the obvious one (you get very sore from sitting on a hard bench), and secondly the spiritual—the natural man aches at the acceptance of Order. But it is not usually in connection with the Fall that we hear of Caucasia. It is more often mentioned as a paradise of rose gardens and Taliessin visiting it (in *The Queen's Servant*) finds that

The lambs

that wander among roses of Caucasia are golden-lamped.
I have seen from its blue skies a flurry of snow
bright as a sudden irrepressible smile
drive across a golden-fleeced landscape.

These marvels, however, are not visible to the *natives* of Caucasia ; only to those who go thither *via* Byzantium.

At the other end of the world is Logres—the brain of the Empire protected by the rocky Hebrides as by a skull, the face of the Empire looking towards Carbonek. It is in the mind, therefore in the head, of Man that Broceliande and Byzantium must be at-oned. In Gaul are the breasts : there, in the University of Paris, arose the bone-building milk of scholastic philosophy. In Italy are the hands : chiefly because Italy means Rome and Rome the Papacy and the Papacy the Mass, ' the heart-breaking manual acts of the Pope '. But those ' manual acts ' are to the poet the consummation of all manual acts— behind them lie the bridge-building which first gave the priests of pagan Rome the name of *pontiffs*, the road-making of the Romans, the nail-making which went to the Passion of Christ. Hands, as we shall see later, are of especial significance to Williams.

But the mention of these ' heart-breaking manual acts ' raises a question. Why is sacrifice necessary ? Why have the palaces of Rome grown pale and turned into churches ? The answer to this lies in the story of the Fall which is given in the seventh strophe. Williams here recapitulates his own version of the story of Genesis, which he has already expounded in prose (*He Came Down from Heaven*, Ch. 2). The Fall was ' an alteration in Knowledge '. God from all eternity knows both good and evil : both the good which He has created and the evil which He has not created. He knows the latter by ' simple intelligence ' without calling it into existence ; knows it as an unrealized contingency. Man's knowledge, however, is limited by experience, and Man therefore at first knew only Good ; there was nothing else for him to know. To the Adam in this blissful condition came the terrible wish to ' know as gods ', to know more than good, to know that contrast of good with evil which God knew as a contingency though not an actuality ;

> Does not God vision the principles at war ?
> Let us grow to the height of God and the Emperor :
> Let us gaze, son of man, on the Acts in contention.

They were able to effect their wish. But knowledge by ' simple intelligence ' was impossible to their nature. For them, to know evil meant to experience evil ; and since nothing but good existed this could only mean to experience good *as* evil. Hence the first result of the Fall was shame—which consisted precisely in experiencing as evil their own bodies which were in fact good : hence, finally, that state of mind in which the Divine Order and God Himself are experienced as evil. The whole universe is thus seen in reversal—'the feet of creation walk backward'. The image of the anti-God (the prince of demons whom a monk saw seated on Justinian's throne, as Gibbon tells us, 'a face without features' or 'a body without a head') is the consummation of this process, the Emperor's opposite—

> Inarticulate always on an inarticulate sea
> beyond P'o-Lu the headless Emperor moves,
> the octopuses round him ; lost are the Roman hands
> lost are the substantial instruments of being.

The short, songful lyric *Taliessin's Return to Logres* shows us the poet retreading the path he had trodden when he met Merlin. Fresh from Byzantium, he is now better able to face the borders of Broceliande and reaches Arthur's camp in safety. There are things in this piece (notably the 'golden sickle') which I do not understand.

Mount Badon must be placed in the imaginary chronology at least several months after the *Return*. Taliessin has had time to win an established position in Logres in the double function of court poet and cavalry officer. We are here dealing with the most historical part of the Arthurian legend—the battle of Mons Badonicus in which Arthur finally defeated the Saxons. For Williams this is, of course, an 'appearance of Byzantium', a triumph of 'the city'. 'The city' is manifested first in 'the civilized single command'; secondly, in the patience of Taliessin—

> all lies in a passion of patience—my lord's rule—

and thirdly, in that image or conceit which occupies most of the poem. While Taliessin waits the moment to advance he sees, far away with his spiritual eye, another poet, the poet *par excel-*

lence of ' the city ', Virgil. Virgil and Taliessin are in a sense doing the same thing ; both are about to impose the city on chaos—Virgil to impose it on the chaos of thought and language by a great line of verse, Taliessin to impose it on the chaos of the battle by a charge. The vision becomes so intense that for one moment we are completely transported to the quiet of the ' trellised path by the sea ' where Virgil is composing, and Mount Badon has receded beyond our horizon—' Barbaric centuries away, the ghostly battle contended '. Next moment we are back with Taliessin in Arthur's line of battle and ' Civilized centuries away, the Roman moved '. The spiritual identity of both moments (for they are one in the throne-room of the Emperor, though far separated when ' phenomenally abated ' by history) is realized when, as it were in a single act, Virgil writes his hexameter on his wax tablet and Taliessin writes his charge on the battle. His spear is his pen ; his charge is the swooping of ' the Aeneid's beaked lines ' ; it is, in a sense, Virgil who is winning the battle. Poetry (' the grand art ') ' masters the thudding hammer of Thor '. On a deeper level still it is the Word, the Risen Lord (described in images borrowed from the Apocalypse) who at this point draws the whole battle into Himself.

The Saxons are crushed, the Arthurian monarchy established. In the next poem, *The Crowning of Arthur*, we see the triumph. Externally all is well : nay, more than well, all is gorgeous. The poem is full of torch-light, flute music, heraldry. The heraldic beasts on the shields, conventionalized into symbols of honour and order, are an expression of the long-desired union between Broceliande and Byzantium—

> Taliessin in the crowd beheld the compelled brutes,
> wildness formalized, images of mathematics.

But the union is precarious. All is not as well as it looks. Merlin, looking down on the pageant from the dome of St. Stephen's, sees it all in the light of Byzantium (' the dome of Sophia ') and can therefore already discern, along with much that is good and fair, the elements of possible corruption. Thus on the one hand he sees the saintly Percivale, sacrificial Bors, the tender self-mocking humility of Dinadan ; on the other he sees the sinister Morgause, sees Guinevere and Lancelot, and, worst of all, the fatal flaw in the king himself. ' The king made for the kingdom, or the kingdom made for the king ? ' That is the question. The right answer has been given in the quotation from Dante's *De Monarchia* prefixed to the whole *Taliessin* volume : ' Hence it is that the proper operation does not exist for the sake of the essence, but the essence has its being for the sake of the operation.' Lovers exist for the sake of love, poets for the sake of poetry, kings for the sake of kingdoms : not *vice versa.* And Arthur is already wrong in heart about this matter. And therefore doom already hangs over Logres. The Empire itself—considered as an earthly expression of the Divine Order—is already endangered ; Sophia therefore already ' beleaguered ', already singing of the Dolorous Blow. On this note of doom, sounding in the midst of splendour and victory, the first movement of the cycle closes.

III

The Golden Age in Logres

LOGRES is now established, and the time for the adventures of the Grail is not yet. If Williams were writing a narrative poem the problem of filling up this interval, or of so passing it over that we should not feel a gap, might be a difficult one. But since he is writing a cycle of lyrics the problem does not arise. He can represent that brief morning of courtesy, poetry, and civilization—that momentary attainment of ' the city '—by dipping into it wherever he chooses. The unity of his work is not a unity of Action in the Aristotelian sense ; rather a unity of thought, temper, and style. First, therefore, we find Taliessin practising his function of court poet. He composes his *Song of the Unicorn*.

It will be remembered that Taliessin, at the very beginning of his career, had foretold that ' no woman would ever wish to bed him '. The poet or, more generally, the man of genius, does not often make a good lover in the ordinary sense. There are no doubt exceptions ; Williams's own brilliantly happy marriage most conspicuous among them. But the list of instances which confirm his theory is long. Genius is ' ill to live with '. Any brisk fellow would have served Fanny Brawne's turn better than Keats. As we read the lives of Hazlitt, Shelley, Coleridge, de Musset, and the like, we cannot help feeling sorry that great men have not more often seen in their genius a vocation to virginity. Taliessin explains the rule, and also why there are exceptions, in the *Song of the Unicorn*. The poet is an oddity. His genius comes from the depth of Nature. It is one of those ' shouldering shapes of the skies of Broceliande ' which are, to the normal Caucasian woman, a mere rumour. The poet, if you will, is a unicorn. Virginity attracts him (as the old Bestiaries said) but he does not attract it. What should a healthy young woman in search of a mate, of children, of an establishment, do with this 'snorting alien love' who comes galloping to her from a horizon which even he 'has no voice to explain'? And in a sense the young woman is quite right. The unicorn does not in the last resort want what alone she has to give. He only wants (gruesome distraction from the real erotic issue!) to polish his horn between her breasts. That is the fatal defect of the genius as lover. He is apt to make of the flesh-and-blood woman a mere starting point for his own visions: to exploit love (hers as well as his) in the interests of his art. That is why she turns from him—as Lesbia turned soon from Catullus—to a 'true man', a gay hunter who knows what he wants, who can defeat the unicorn in a moment and hang its head ('the cuckold of the wood') on the very tree beneath which he embraces the girl.

That conclusion is right and proper. Taliessin sings it with a wry smile perhaps, but with no bitterness. And yet... and yet... there is another possible conclusion. If any woman will endure the unicorn's love she will indeed suffer: but she will become the Mother of his Voice. Some great work of art which encircles the city of men and which (sharp as horn, deep as blood, wide as the ocean or the lightning flash) combines the tempestuous Broceliandic shapes and the exact spiritual sciences, will be her son. It is usually better that these nuptials should remain intellectual. Would Beatrice have borne *The Divine Comedy* to Dante if they had been married?

While Taliessin sings thus of his own destiny other and more ordinary loves are going on in the court. They go on indeed partly because he so sings. In the very next poem (*Bors to Elayne : the Fish of Broceliande*) we see how this happens. Bors is no unicorn: at his last appearance in the cycle we see him as a husband and father praying 'for the need and the bliss of his household'. But Taliessin has in one sense fathered Bors's love: as Bors says to Elayne—

> In the great hall's glow
> Taliessin sang of the sea-rooted western wood ;
> his song meant all things to all men, and you to me.

It will be remembered that in an earlier note Williams has said that all Broceliande is ' felt in the beloved '. To Bors, therefore, gazing for the first time on Elayne, it is natural that a poem of the ' sea-rooted western wood ' should instantaneously make itself a poem about her. And yet, next moment, how absurd ! What can be less alike than this lady and Broceliande with all its monstrous beasts and birds ? Bors corrects himself. It is not that Elayne is like Broceliande : it is rather that he, in the presence of Elayne, has found love in Broceliande—at least in a stream that was flowing towards it. He does not use the word ' love ' of course : who, at that moment of first vision, ever did ? He only knows that something incomparably bright, elusive, and living has darted into his experience ; —a Broceliandic fish. It seems to him at one moment something that is coming from the Lady to him, at another something going from him to the Lady. He must offer it to her. And yet, as their hands meet, as it darts up her arm, it will be lost again. It has flashed back to its true home (for we were right after all —of course, of course she *is* Broceliande) to vanish in those swirling streams, round a boulder, down a cataract, ' back to its haunt in a fathomless bottomless pool '. What is it—this thing flashing between them which is neither spirit nor sense as either has been known till that moment ? Nimue may know ; but woe to those mortals who trust any psychologist or moralist or even any other pair of lovers to tell them. There is only one way to find out. These two must try together that great experiment, must become that double-natured creature, that ' one flesh ' which alone can utter the secret name of their love. But even if they can call it from its stream, even if it comes flashing to them from the ' aboriginal main ' its ambiguity will still dazzle them. It seems to shoot onward in two different and even contradictory directions, one leading to ' the smooth plane of the happy flesh ' But the other ends where the Fish as an anagram of Christ stands over some martyr's grave in the catacombs. On a simple level this paradox can be fairly easily grasped : Love leads to pleasure and to sacrifice. But the poet also means that when the two lovers become 'a twy-nature' (one organism in two sexes) they are a living symbol of the grand Twy-Nature, Christ (the union of God and Man in one Person) who alone can utter celestial, as they utter earthly, love. The conceit is of course facilitated by the early Christian use of the fish as a cryptogram.

The poem ends with Bors offering—or receiving, for the two here are indistinguishable—the 'fish'. The two lovers know now the depth that lives and moves beneath all possible Camelots—

Everywhere the light through the great leaves is blown.

These two pieces introduce us to Williams's doctrine of Love. On this subject, as on so many others, he reaffirms the Romantic tradition but continues and elaborates it in modes that amount to a correction of earlier Romanticism. His most systematic statements in prose are to be found in the fifth chapter of *He Came Down from Heaven* and in *The Figure of Beatrice*. His master is Dante. Love means to him something that begins with what he calls a 'Beatrician experience'—the sort of experience that Dante records in the *Vita Nuova*. There are, he is careful to point out, other similar experiences which do not involve a Lady; Wordsworth's vision of Nature is an example. This has not yet lasted in the world so long as the erotic kind, and it is with the latter that Williams is concerned.

The Beatrician experience may be defined as the recovery (in respect to one human being) of that vision of reality which would have been common to all men in respect to all things if Man had never fallen. The lover sees the Lady as the Adam saw all things before they foolishly chose to experience good as evil, to 'gaze upon the acts in contention'. Williams believes that this experience is what it professes to be. The 'light' in which the beloved appears to be clothed is true light; the intense significance which she appears to have is not an illusion; in her (at that moment) Paradise is actually revealed, and in the lover Nature is renovated. The great danger is lest he should mistake the vision, which is really a starting point, for a goal ; lest he should mistake the vision of Paradise for arrival there. He must follow this road till it leads him to the Byzantine precision. The immediate glory will dazzle him ' unless he has a mind *to examine the pattern* of the glory ' (*He Came Down from Heaven*, p. 95, italics mine). He must learn ' the Theology of Romantic Love ' instead of amusing himself with its ' fables ' and ' superstitions '. It is ' the effort after the pattern ' that makes the difference ; for ' the superstitions make heaven and earth in the form of the beloved ' whereas ' the theology declares that the beloved is the first preparatory form of heaven and earth '. The Beatrician experience, like the Wordsworthian experience, is the summons to a discipline and a way of life—the long way recorded in the *Divine Comedy* or *The Prelude*.

The Beatrician experience does not usually last : [1] nor, it will be remembered, did the Wordsworthian. Dante's Beatrice died —but even had she lived the story would have been much the same. The glory is temporary ; in that sense Beatrice nearly always dies. But a transitory vision is not necessarily a vision of the transitory. That it passes does not prove it a hallucination. It has in fact been a glimpse of what is eternally real. The phenomenal Beatrice—Beatrice as she is in this fallen world— has for an instant been identical with the real Beatrice—Beatrice as she (and all things) will be seen to be, and always to have been, when we reach the throne-room at Byzantium. The precise moment at which the phenomenal Beatrice loses her identity with the real one is a repetition of the Fall, as Palomides discovers in a later poem when

> division stretched between
> The Queen's identity and the Queen.

At that moment all sorts of false paths lie open to the lover— rage, resentment, infidelity, or the contented decline into humdrum concupiscence. But the true road is the long Dantean

[1] Williams, according to Fr. Matthew, thought it normally, but not inevitably, transient.

pilgrimage ' from world to world ', up the steep mountain to the place where Beatrice says once more ' Look on me well. I am, I am Beatrice.'

But something even more troublesome than this withdrawal must be faced. Not only does the glory fade away from one Lady : it may, more disturbingly, reappear in another. Cynics have hailed this as one more proof that the first appearance was an illusion : eulogists of romantic love have too often tried to hush it up. According to Williams we must do neither of these things. Nothing must ever be hushed up ; the road to Byzantium is one of increasing awareness, vigilance, attention. If the first appearance of the glory revealed one being as all beings really and eternally are, then it ought to be expected that the glory might return to reveal similar transcendental truth about some other being.

' The second image is not to be denied ; we are not to pretend it is not there, or indeed to diminish its worth ; we are only asked to free ourselves from concupiscence in regard to it. . . . The first image was towards physical union ; the second towards its separation. It repeats the first, in an opposite direction. But both movements are alike intense towards most noble Love.' (*Figure of Beatrice*, p. 49.)

Romantic Love is neither necessarily joined to bodily fruition nor necessarily abstracted from it : the way to which the glory invites us may run through marriage or it may not. Unless it were possible—and heavenly—to be enamoured of the glory without desiring the woman, how should we ever grow mature for the life of heaven where that glory in its fullest meridian blaze will clothe every woman and every man, every beast, blade of grass, rock ? (' In the third heaven the stones of the waste glimmer like summer stars.') Admittedly this movement of romantic love is difficult ; jealousy contributes to that difficulty quite as much as concupiscence and is (however dangerous the admission may be) no less horrible a sin.

But at this point we must guard against a misunderstanding. To say that the lover, in certain circumstances, must turn away

from concupiscence is not to say that his attention should be
diverted from the beloved's body. There is no question here of
the so-called ' Platonic ' solution ; of loving the lady's soul
instead of her person. The distinction of soul and body is forever impossible in the Beatrician experience : that is the very
schism which the experience momentarily heals. The essence
of the glory is that it appears in the flesh : more shortly, that it
appears. Hence in the next poem, *Taliessin in the School of the
Poets*, we are invited to study the human body. The King's
poet comes to visit the bardic school at Camelot. It is apparently
a summer day, the pigeons cooing in the courtyard. As Taliessin
stands in the doorway with hot sunlight behind him his shadow
falls upon and slightly overlaps the golden figure of Phoebus
which lies on the floor of the school as a brass lies on a church
floor. Phoebus, the god of poetry and of the sun, is there
shown trampling the ' mud-born Python ' and at the same time
catching the whole universe in the net of his light—an instance
of the victory of the city. The young poets, busied with the
paraphernalia of poetry (which in that age was almost a depart-
ment of magic) look up from their parchments and vellums,
their scrolls of prophecy and ritual, at the human body of
Phoebus. Taliessin, striding to the chief place in the school
(' the sovereign chair ') bursts into song : such a cryptic song
as a master of bards, addressing bards, might be supposed to sing.
Its subject is the human body. The poet begins by praising all
delicate and exact things ; the gold on butterflies' wings (their
flight would be ruined if the Creator's brush had spilled on them
never so little more or less of the splendour), the hazel measuring-
rod, the light on the nape of a neck. Then he proceeds to
construct the body as if it were a geometrical diagram. At the
bottom of this page my note, transcribed from Williams, runs,
' the body, of which the centre line is given, obviously, and yet
never quite given '. That is the key to his whole conception of
the body : it is an ideal geometry mediated through an actual
arrangement of living curves. The ' head-to-heel ' line and the
line of the outspread arms are as the two intersecting diameters

of a sphere : the ' rondures ' of the caucasian base derive their significance (as pattern) from the ' absolute ' spine. But all this geometry is flushed with living glory, ' creamed with crimson ' and ' grace-pricked to gules ' by the heart. There is indeed no fathoming the bloom of a fair body in this fallen world ; dullness and concupiscence in turn or even (at times) in unison conspire to blind us. It can be fully understood only *sub specie aeternitatis* by those who fly up the porphyry stair into the presence of the Emperor. For there, at the Centre, all things that here are remote and diverse from one another, and all in infinite strength, come together, drawn from the far blue distances. Their reconciliation is not one of compromise : each is itself to the *n*th when they meet—so favoured, so ' indulged ' is that ' Byzantine floor '. Everything turns out to be equally central when we see it in the full light of the Unity—' each moment there is the midmost '. Mere instinct is no longer separable from Grace, nor wonder from will, nor love from merit nor simple seeing from discipline. So at Byzantium ; but here in Logres it is not so. Here body and spirit, Broceliande and the Empire, are not, or not yet, at-oned. There is still contrast between the straight Roman roads and the tribal tracks, the cut hazels (rods of measurement, punishment, incantation) and the wild hazels by the roadside.

The song ends. The darker theme which is to occupy us in the next poem becomes audible. Taliessin's voice sharpens ; he is thinking of Virgil. More exactly, he is thinking of *Aeneid VI*. He is thinking of Palinurus who died with no more reward for all his wanderings than ' Italy seen from a wave ' (*prospexi Italiam summa sublimis ab unda*, 357). Then, following Virgil deeper into that book, into the lower world, he ' defines the organisms of hell '. Uneasiness is creeping over the school of the poets. The King's falcons stir on their perches. Taliessin's voice has become harsh. He cries out that the flood of great verse is stemmed by death and staled by repetition, that poetry plunges at last into the void. As Taliessin speaks the young poets see the universe drawn into the design of Phoebus and Python on the floor : but it is a universe that breathes a universal sigh, like the sigh of the ghosts in *Aeneid VI* stretching out their arms on the shore of an unpassable river.

The darker theme, still unexplained, dies away. Already in a previous stanza visions have begun to accompany Taliessin's song. The golden ' brass ' has been coloured by his song. Many-lined patterns, all of red, glide through the room : they open, infinitely numerous, in the high seat of the chief bard. But all are dominated by, or summed up in, the human figure of Phoebus. The ' crowned form of anatomized man ' is the pattern of patterns. The young poets, gazing at it, ' study precision ' : their master sighs, ' Lord, save us '.

What was the meaning of the sudden gloom which dashed Taliessin in the midst of his high hymn to the human body ? In the next piece (*Taliessin on the Death of Virgil*) we are given the answer. In the first poem of all, *The Calling of Taliessin*, we have already seen how fully Williams realizes, as perhaps only great poets do, that poetry is after all only poetry. It is not a substitute for philosophy or theology, much less for sanctification. Not even Virgil can be saved by poetry. That is the real meaning of the images in the preceding piece. It is Virgil himself who died without reaching the *patria*, who saw ' Italy ' only from a wave before he was engulfed forever. It is Virgil himself who stretches out his hands among the ghosts *ripae ulterioris amore*, longing to pass a river that he cannot pass. This poet from whose work so many Christians have drawn spiritual nourishment was not himself a Christian—did not himself know the full meaning of his own poetry, for (in Keble's fine words) ' thoughts beyond their thought to those high bards were given '. That is the exquisite cruelty ; he made honey not for himself ; he helped to save others, himself he could not save.

The simplicity of Williams's thought here will shock many readers. We are back in the world of Dante and Langland. The problem of the virtuous Pagan is for him a real one. The fact that Virgil was a great poet does not in the least alter the fact that he cannot have had Christian faith, hope, and charity, without which no man can be saved. 'Everything is itself and not some other thing.'

The poem falls into two parts. The first is a description (one of the most accurate I know) of the moment at which consciousness crumbles, that moment which most of us have known in high fever or at the beginning of anaesthesia. Virgil's death, it is suggested, was like that. Every possible grip has failed. The two things he loved, Rome and Augustus, have become, the one a nonentity, the other a swelling, gruesome, obscene, gargantuan shape. The life-long metre, the hexameter, is a 'meaningless sweet sound': those who have known how a metre, after all sense has been emptied out of it, can torment the brain, will understand. Virgil is overwhelmed in the mere flotsam and rubble of what had been his own poetic universe,

> all the shapes of his labour,
> his infinite images, dropping pell-mell.

And that, as far as Nature goes, would have been the end of the story. But the second part tells that as Virgil was about to perish in the 'perpetual falling, perpetual burying' helpers rushed towards him, dived beneath him, caught him as he fell. They had rushed from what was (to him) the far future, for this transaction is outside time. All who have been or will be nurtured by Virgil's hexameters rushed back along the timeless corridors to save their 'master and friend', the 'holy poet', to place at his service the faith which they had and he lacked. As they in Christ, so he in the Christ in them, tasted the 'largesse' of 'the land of the Trinity'. But even then the delicate courtesy of the spiritual world rules that they approach him not as teachers but as pupils. They ask pardon for the 'excellent absurdity' of appearing, on that one occasion, as the fathers of their poetical father and carrying what has so long carried them—

> what salvation
> may reign here by us, deign of good will to endure.

It is important to realize that this passage is not simply a poetic conceit. Williams has said here nothing that he is not prepared to avouch in cool prose : and the whole chapter on ' The Practice of Substituted Love ' in *He Came Down from Heaven* is devoted to the exposition of it. The doctrine, which he called that of Exchange or Substitution, may be summed up in three propositions. (1) The Atonement was a Substitution, just as Anselm said. But that Substitution, far from being a mere legal fiction irrelevant to the normal workings of the universe, was simply the supreme instance of a universal law. ' He saved others, himself he cannot save ' is a *definition* of the Kingdom. All salvation, everywhere and at all times, in great things or in little, is vicarious. The courtesy of the Emperor has absolutely decreed that no man can paddle his own canoe and every man can paddle his fellow's, so that the shy offering and modest acceptance of indispensable aid shall be the very form of the celestial etiquette. (2) We can and should ' bear one another's burdens ' in a sense much more nearly literal than is usually dreamed of. Any two souls can (' under the Omnipotence ') make an agreement to do so : the one can offer to take another's shame or anxiety or grief and the burden will actually be trans-ferred. This Williams most seriously maintained, and I have reason to believe that he spoke from experimental knowledge. (3) Such ' exchanges ', however, are not made only by mutual compact. We can be their beneficiaries without our own knowledge or consent, as when our god-parents became our substitutes at the font. Such is the coinherence of all souls that they are not even limited by Time. Hence in *Descent into Hell* —a story which shows the doctrine of Exchange in action— the heroine takes upon herself the terror of a remote ancestor and liberates him from feeling it. The present poem means what it says. I think the poet would have said in so many words, if asked, that any Christian Virgilian can this very night assist in the salvation of Virgil.

From these mysteries and the complex lyrical metres in which they are expressed we turn abruptly to a simpler and a less fortunate figure and to the marching lilt of rough octosyllabics.

Palomides the Saracen Knight, the unsuccessful lover of Iseult, comes out of Mohammedan Spain ' through the green-pennon-skirted Pyrenees' and the ' cross-littered land of Gaul' to Cornwall and the house of King Mark. The anachronism whereby Islam is made contemporary with Arthur is deliberate : Islam was for Williams the symbol (as it is certainly the greatest historical expression) of something which is eternally the opposite of Sarras and Carbonek. Islam denies the Incarnation. It will not allow that God has descended into flesh or that Manhood has been exalted into Deity. It is

> the sharp curved line of the Prophet's blade
> that cuts the Obedience from the Obeyed.

It stands for all religions that are afraid of matter and afraid of mystery, for all misplaced reverences and misplaced purities that repudiate the body and shrink back from the glowing materialism of the Grail. It stands for what Williams called ' heavy morality '—the ethics of sheer duty and obedience as against the shy yet (in the long run) shameless acceptance of heaven's courtesies flowing from the ' homely and courteous lord '. It is strong, noble, venerable ; yet radically mistaken. It had nibbled at Christianity almost from the beginning in the swarm of heresies which denied the full doctrine of Incarnation. That is the point of the Prelude to *The Region of the Summer Stars*. St. Paul preached ' the golden Ambiguity '—the irony beyond all ironies which the manger in the Bethlehem stable presents, the ' physiological glory '. But the ' ancient intellect ' shrank back from the new doctrine,

> The converted doctors turned to their former confessions,
> the limitary heresiarchs feared the indiscretions of matter . . .
> Professing only a moral union they fled
> from the new-spread bounty.

The Prelude to *Taliessin through Logres* is also concerned with this conflict between the ' ambiguity ' of Incarnation and the heavy lucidity of mere Monotheism. On the historical level it is a fact that ' the Moslem stormed Byzantium '. On the spiritual level huge areas of the world fell back from the subtler and more ' scandalous ' Faith—and fall back daily in the sub-Christian doctrines of Christ's person which are dear to the modern world. This is not the defeat of truth by simple error or of good by simple evil : it is the loss of living, paradoxical, vibrant, mysterious truths in obvious and petrifying truths (for mere Monotheism blinds and stifles the mind like noonday sun in the Arabian deserts till we may well ' call on the hills to hide us '). It is the defeat of fine and tender and even frolic delicacies of goodness by iron legalism, the ' fallacy of rational virtue '. Islam is true so far as it affirms : we must rejoice that it conquered the old Dualism of Persia. But it affirms unity in such a way that ' union is breached ' ; and then, however truly and with whatever grandeur the muezzin cried ' Good is God ',

> Lost is the light on the hills of Caucasia,
> glory of the Emperor, glory of substantial being.

Palomides journeys through Gaul. Knowing already ' the measurement of man ' he knows that in Christendom something more complex can be learned—' the height of God-in-man '. On Lateran, that is on Mons Coelia the reputed home of Coelius Vibenna, leader of those notorious sorcerers the pre-Roman Etruscans, the Church is established. But Palomides is bound for Britain. It had been discovered by Caesar at some period after the end of the Etruscan ' magic ' and before the exposition of the Christian ' mystery ' ; discovered as the reality behind old Gallic legends of a land to which dead men's ghosts were ferried westward. What awaits Palomides there is his first sight of Iseult.

What we are now going to witness is a Beatrician experience going wrong. There is no mistake about its Beatrician quality ; indeed nowhere, in my opinion, has the poet expressed so perfectly what he had to say about the human body. It is Iseult's bare arm that sums up all : there Palomides sees in a flash

> how curves of golden life define
> the straightness of a perfect line . . .
> where well might Archimedes prove
> the doctrine of Euclidean love.

An outstretched arm is, so to speak, straighter than straightness itself : the very curves define its invisible straightness. Its curves are richer than any curves we can find in cloud or water or silk ; the very straightness rounds them. For one moment while Palomides thus sees Queen Iseult all discords are resolved. His ' mind ' completely obeys both his ' blood ' and the objective fact : his blood equally obeys fact and mind ; the fact itself is intensely and incredibly obedient to mind and blood. But there are only two fortunate sequels to such an experience : either a love consummated in the flesh or the long pilgrimage of Dante to ' intellectual nuptials '. Of the first Palomides has no chance : the queen sits between her husband Mark and her lover Tristram. For the second he is not prepared. He gazes for one dangerous moment too long, gazes while the vision fades into a different kind of vision. Between Iseult seen in God and the merely actual Iseult separation has occurred : her arm lay ' empty of glory '. It was at that moment that Palomides' life-long monomaniac pursuit of the Questing Beast began. He heard it somewhere in the roof—scratching itself

> in the blank between
> The Queen's substance and the Queen.

The entrance of the Beast is connected with Iseult's husband and her lover—the husband who tossed the Saracen poet a ring to pay for the song, and the lover with whom she smiled and talked. It is primarily a jealous beast. Palomides continues to gaze on Iseult after the ' celestial light ' has faded from her. While the vision lasted he was a romantic lover, and free as such to accept the ' pattern ' which in his case, as in Dante's, excluded bodily fruition. But he continues to gaze on what is now 'the light of common day'. What might for romantic love have been one kind of success is for workaday desire mere frustration. Carnal jealousy awakes. It is the enemy Palomides must henceforth deal with ; he has embraced his Quest. We shall see later into what regions it led him.

The Beginning of Separations

L AMORACK *and the Queen Morgause of Orkney* draws together into one vision all evils and all threats of evil that there are in Logres. In the first place it sets before us a fact about human passion which has not yet appeared in the poem. Not all loves—not even all life-long loves—begin with a Beatrician experience. Men can love, even to death and dishonour, that which they have never seen ' apparelled in celestial light ', that which, even from the first moment, they have feared and in a sense hated. Lamorack has loved Morgause from the first day he saw her : he has never liked her. He does not even think her, in any ordinary sense, beautiful. She is the most Celtic, and the most terrible, person in the poem. Her nearest kinswoman in poetry is that Scotch queen Aoife who bore to Cuchulain the son whom Cuchulain killed.[1] Yeats has painted her

> there was one
> In Scotland, where you had learnt the trade of war,
> That had a stone-pale cheek and red-brown hair—

a suitable mistress for one who held Cuchulain's views of love

> I never have known love but as a kiss
> In the mid-battle, and a difficult truce
> Of oil and water, candles and dark night,
> Hillside and hollow, the hot-footed sun,
> And the cold, sliding, slippery-footed moon—
> A brief forgiveness between opposites
> That have been hatreds for three times the age
> Of this long-'stablished ground.

Aoife was stone-pale : but Morgause is more like the spirit of stone itself—not, to be sure, of stone considered as a cold thing,

---

[1] She may owe something to Swinburne's sketch of the same character in *Tristram of Lyonesse*, I.

but of stone considered as pressure, sharpness, ruthlessness :
stone the record of huge passions in Earth's depth. He sees
her first among the outer islands—

> the roar
> of the ocean beyond all coasts threatened on one hand ;
> on the other we saw the cliffs of Orkney stand.
> Caves and hollows in the crags were filled with the scream
> of seamews nesting and fleeting ; the extreme theme
> of Logres rose in harsh cries and hungry storms,
> and there, hewn in a cleft, were hideous huge forms.

On such an island, herself like that island, her eyes first met his ;
and it was like a second Fall of Man, a second emergence of
those exorbitant natures which Adam's desire to see the Acts
in Contention evoked. The sea wind was whipping her hair
about her face : yet the face ' outstripped her hair '. One has
seen faces with that quality : however they may be at rest in
space, violent speed is embodied in them.   And as in some women
things not in themselves beautiful—a husky voice, a face continually wreathed by drollery—may become almost obsessively
attractive, so with Morgause ; the frightful energy of passion, the
murderous danger, the fierce simplicities, of her face claim their
slave at the first interchange of glances.   As Lamorack says

> Her hand discharged catastophe ; I was thrown
> before it ; I saw the source of all stone,
> the rigid tornado, the schism and first strife
> of primeval rock with itself, Morgause Lot's wife.

The suggestion, in the last words, of that other Lot's wife who
became a pillar of salt, is doubtless intended : there is, if I may
so put it, a *mineral* quality in Morgause. The last stanza in
which Lamorack's life-long passion is affirmed in joyless words
gives the natural result of his first meeting with her. The heavy
fetters of an obsession may prove even more lasting than the
' golden snare ' of Euclidean, poetic, and intellectual love.

This is Lamorack's personal tragedy : with it are mixed two
tragedies darker still. Returned from the northern islands, he

finds his terrible mistress seated in Arthur's hall. She was Arthur's half-sister, she was there with her husband and her sons, herself seated on the king's left while Guinevere sat on his right ; all is, superficially, suitable and friendly. But Lamorack sees in her eyes the same hideous half-humanised shapes which he had seen carved on the Orkney cliffs ; he hears again the screaming of the sea-mews. And well he may. For with this sister Arthur has committed incest—not knowing who she was, intending only fornication. And now she bears unborn in her body the king's son—Mordred who betrayed and killed him. In order to commit his smaller, his intended, sin Arthur had gone into a place of darkness, had—in a sense deliberately—gone where men know not what they are doing. Into a dark place which was something like a cave and something like a tavern, and something like a mere arch at the side of a street—into a ' wine-wide cell, an open grave ' he had gone as a ' man without eyes ' so as not to see that the woman's face was the image of his own face. For that is the horror of incest : it offends against the law of exchange, the strain gives itself not to another strain but only back to itself. It is a physiological image of that far more abominable incest which—calling it Gomorrah—Williams studies in *Descent into Hell* : that final rejection of all exchange whereby the heart turns to the *succubus* it has itself engendered. In such a place Mordred was begotten on ' the shape of a blind woman under the shape of a blind man ' ; God's prohibition ' half-formed ', almost invisible in the rock wall above them. This moment shares with one other the dishonour of having frustrated the whole design of Logres and foiled the work of the Grail ; and the other was curiously like it. Morgause and Arthur were sister and brother, Balin and Balan were brother and brother. Both pairs were blind and ignorant ; Balin killed Balan, un-knowingly—as he also, unknowingly, struck the Dolorous Blow and hindered the coming of the Grail. Yet not quite innocently ; if he had not been Balin *le sauvage* he would not perhaps have done either—even as Arthur, had he been chaste, would not have begotten Mordred.

With the begetting of Mordred and the striking of the Dolorous Blow all is lost—

> The child lies unborn in the queen's womb ;
> unformed in his brain is the web of all our doom,
> as unformed in the minds of all the great lords
> lies the image of the split Table and of surreptitious swords.

And all these things are so because Man is fallen. The lust and fierceness of Morgause, the lust and weakness of Arthur, the folly of Balin, the treachery of Mordred, are all specimens of those ' contingent ' things which God knew but would not create and which the foolish Adam insisted on experiencing. Sometimes, before they appear on earth in human actions and characters, they have been anticipated on another plane—evoked as phantoms by sorcerers like Coelius Vibenna or carved in stone by devil-worshippers, as Lamorack sees them carved (' hideous, huge forms ') on the walls of Orkney. Seeing them, he knows at once that they are things which only the Emperor should have known—

> before the making of man or beast
> the Emperor knew all carved contingent shapes.

But this terrible knowledge has, at Man's own invitation, descended on Man.

> Sideways in the cleft they lay, and the seamews' wings
> everywhere flying, or the mist, or the mere slant of the things
> seemed to stir them.

Then, as storm burst and the ship fled before it from the islands, these ' giant inhuman forms ' seemed to be loosed from their places, to follow them in the air, stone no more but now spirit and now, when Lamorack returned from the sea to Arthur's hall, no longer spirit but fully incarnate in Morgause, and soon to be more fully incarnate still in her son Mordred.

The whole poem marks strongly the difference between the technique of narrative or drama and that of the metaphysical ode.

The obsessive love of Lamorack, which is what a dramatist would seize on, though vividly imagined, is used by Williams chiefly as the medium through which to show us the

> contingent knowledge of the Emperor floating into sight.

His concern is not with the psychological origins of evil but with its metaphysical ' procession ', its intrusion from nightmare into reality, the horrible stages whereby what ought not to be at all becomes an image, and what ought to be only an image becomes stone, and what ought to be only stone becomes a woman, and what ought to be only a woman becomes her son. For the whole tendency of Williams's myth of the Fall is to make us feel evil not as imperfection, nor even as revolt, but as miscreation— the bringing to be of what must not (and even in a sense cannot) be, yet now it is : as though monstrous members, horns, trunks, feelers, tusks, were sprouting out of the body.

Meanwhile, what does all this mean for the ordinary life of Logres ? At first sight—down on that lower level—you would say that all was still going well. In the household of Bors, now married to Elayne, all is going well in fact. The word *lady* means loaf-giver. Elayne and her women are dealing out bread to the fieldsmen as Bors (in *Bors to Elayne : on the King's Coins*) comes back to his house. As he looks at her he remembers that some poet has likened her hair to corn. It will do well enough for a mere artist thinking about colours ; but ' his heart counts the doctrine ', and for the heart the real likeness to corn is in her face, for it is the bread on which his heart lives. Her face —and her hands, hands that bake and distribute bread for others whose hands drain marshes and drive furrows ; hands whose kneading, manipulating thumbs are ' muscled with the power of goodwill ' ; hands which are the instruments of alms and courtesy. Yes : inside this house all is very well. But outside, a different code of Exchange has just come into existence. We are to suppose that since the collapse of the Roman rule Britain has been without coinage, has lived by barter. Now Arthur has set up a mint. The bright new coins (apparently they have the king's head on one side and a dragon on the other) already ' scuttle and scurry between towns and towns '—

> The long file of their snouts crosses the empire,
> and the other themes acknowledge our King's head.

Bors does not question the utility of the new coins ; but he has had bad dreams about them. He has dreamed that ' they teemed ' (i.e. brought forth young)—that money has bred money. He has seen house roofs creaking and breaking under the weight. From this nightmare of live minerals he comes back to Elayne, saying

> mother of children, redeem the new law.

There is, in fact, danger in money. Kay, the boor ' wise in economics ' does not see the danger. He is unreservedly delighted with the idea of a common ' medium of exchange ' between ' London and Omsk ' and a method of controlling the world which will, no doubt, prove ' smoother ' than ' the swords of lords or the orisons of nuns '. But the danger which is hidden from the economist Kay is very clear to the poet Taliessin, Coins are symbols : and being a poet he knows much more about symbols than Kay. A symbol has a life of its own. An *escaped* metaphor—escaped from the control of the total poem or philosophy in which it belongs—may be a poisonous thing. Has Kay considered whether these metal symbols, these metaphors in gold and silver, may not also have a life of their own ? Will money be man's servant—or has it, perhaps, its own views ?

> Sir, if you made verse you would doubt symbols.
> I am afraid of the little loosed dragons.
> When the means are autonomous, they are deadly . . .

The exchanges made by this new medium may prove to be a mere parody of that true exchange whose doctrine the Archbishop now rehearses to the lords—

> the everlasting house the soul discovers
> is always another's ; we must lose our own ends ;
> we must always live in the habitation of our lovers,
> my friend's shelter for me, mine for him.

Such good exchange is not confined to what we call ' the spiritual level '; perhaps nothing truly spiritual ever is. On the fleshly level too it holds good : the exchange of one kind of service for another—Elayne and her women baking what the men have sown and harvested—is honourable and blessed. Nor can we deny that this exchange is facilitated by money. But then money becomes so easily ' autonomous '. We speak (or our fathers spoke) of money as giving an ' independence '—that is, a deadly oblivion of the fact that we all live in and on each other, a deadly illusion that the laws of the city permit independence. Hence the dilemma—' What without coinage or with coinage can be saved ? ' The city by reason of its legitimate complexity, does really need instruments such as coinage which themselves need to be continually redeemed if they are not to become deadly. Civilization is commanded, yet civilization can safely be practised only by those to whom it is promised that ' if they drink any deadly thing it shall not hurt them '. Law can only kill till gospel comes to transcend it, the king's head on the coins is a death's head unless the economic life is ruled by the spirit which rules Elayne. More generally still, every Logres whereof history holds record, can only attain a ' fallacy of rational virtue ' and generate Mordreds in its dark womb unless the Grail comes to it. Therefore, in the meantime,

> Pray, mother of children, pray for the coins,
> pray for Camelot, pray for the king, pray.

All this is sufficiently ominous ; but in the next poem, *The Star of Percivale*, we are happily reminded of the complexity of the real world. Inside the growing failure of Logres something else is springing up. It will be remembered that Merlin, at his first meeting with Taliessin, had hinted as much. Logres might perish, but even then there would be a work for the ' king's poet's household ' to do. We touch here upon one of Williams's fundamental principles. It might be illustrated from the whole history of Judaism and Christianity. Israel is always failing, but there is always a ' remnant ' left ; out of that failure at its nadir, and that remnant at its smallest, salvation flows. It might be illustrated on a homelier level by Chesterton's maxim that ' the success of the marriage springs out of the failure of the honeymoon '. For Williams himself, as we see in *He Came Down from Heaven*, the chosen example is the story of Cain and Abel. Cain has carefully and, no doubt, laudably, prepared an altar and a sacrifice, but no fire descends on it. The fire descends elsewhere, on his brother's altar. Cain fails to understand that this, far from being a hideous anomaly, is one of the laws of the City. ' Unless devotion is given to a thing which must prove false in the end, the thing that is true in the end cannot enter.' ' The way must be made ready for heaven, and then it will come by some other ; the sacrifice must be made ready, and the fire will strike on another altar.' Cain did not understand that ' the very purpose of his offering was to make his brother's accept-able '. And this is what nearly always happens. The thing which we thought principally intended (but how can Omnipotence intend any one thing more than any other ?) comes to nought ; what seems to us a mere by-product (but what could be a by-product to Omniscience ?) bursts into flower. Thus to those who wish to stand on their merits the course of destiny must always seem a horrible celestial sarcasm on their repeated failures : but to those who have been set free by ' the doctrine of largesse ' it will be an ' excellent absurdity', a tender mockery dancing or flickering like summer lightning on what, but for this, they might in some fatal and portentous fashion have regarded as their successes. Once you have grasped the principle it is not chastening but liberating to know that one has always been almost wholly superfluous ; wherever one has done well some other has done all the real work . . . you will do the same for him, perhaps, another day, but you will not know it—' My friend's shelter for me, mine for him.'

Out of the failure of Logres comes—and could not have come otherwise—the strange mode of courtesy called ' the king's poet's household '. Percivale stands at the western door playing his harp. Taliessin, outside in the court, sings to that music.

That is, if you will, he ' steals ' Percivale's music and in that sense ' plays a borrowed harp ', uses a harp which another man is playing—living as all artists do in another's house of art. The ' excellent absurdity ' decrees that the reward should fall not to Percivale but to Taliessin : even as Shakespeare's blank verse fills the world while that of Surrey, the inventor, is forgotten. Taliessin's song lifts to her feet a barbarian slave girl ; she comes running to him in adoration. It is a thing that happens every day. The girl has had a Beatrician experience. In her untaught soul it becomes hero-worship, ' calf-love '—can become whatever Taliessin chooses to make it ; that is why a poet, a musician, an actor, has such advantage as a seducer if he wishes to adopt the role. What Taliessin actually does is telescoped for the purposes of the poem into a matter of minutes : in real life it would, I suppose (but Williams knew better than I) take a few weeks. At such a juncture, paradise being momentarily revealed to the girl, a touch will divert her worship to the true goal. He has no need to snub her or to give her sensible advice. Because he already shows her Paradise she must believe his definition of it. In her passion of obedience, to turn from him, from his voice to the vision it conveyed, is really to remain with him. To obey Another is to obey him. She receives divine grace : none the less because she is bearing ' the light of another ' as he, after all, bore ' the song of another '. She is converted, saved in a labyrinth of vicariousness, ' a tangle of compensations, every joint a centre '. She has entered on the New Life. It will not necessarily be for her a celibate one. Taliessin has taught her the *ars honeste amandi* : another will (under the Omnipotence) reap the harvest.

The Archbishop, passing on his way to Mass, sees in her face that she has seen ' the light of Christ's glory ' : for a moment he ' wears her joy ' (as she wears Taliessin's who wears Percivale's, and all, Christ's). But inside, in the chapel, as they kneel at the Mass, Balin feels only his anger, Arthur worships only himself, Lancelot only the queen.

The Ascent of the Spear continues to show us Taliessin working at his spiritual vocation. The same slave girl who was so suddenly converted in the preceding poem has relapsed—has brawled in the palace, taken a cudgel to a fellow servant, and been duly clapped in the stocks, where she sits ' veined with fury her forehead ' in black, blind rage against all the world. She snaps currishly at Taliessin himself when he approaches her. He talks to her in a style which might easily be mistaken for affectation ; talks as if the flushed, scowling, resentful creature were a great queen and he at once her courtier and her lover. It is not affectation because in a certain sense these are their relations. Only yesterday they have adored together. They have been in Paradise. She had, for a moment and without full understanding, seen him with unfallen vision : but it is Taliessin's privilege both as a poet and as one who will enjoy no woman's love in the flesh to enjoy that vision almost continually, to see that light resting on innumerable faces—hers, not least. In his reconquest of her barbarian soul there are two stages. The first merely removes her resentment, brings her to admit the rightness of the official punishment. The second defeats a much subtler pride. Kay, the Steward, seeing that the girl seems to be a friend of Taliessin's, sends a message offering to release her. The pride that refuses pardon—subtler than the pride that resents punishment—takes a few moments to subdue. Then all is well. The whole episode may be regarded as Williams's answer to those who ask whether the conversion that comes by a Beatrician experience (or in any other sudden flash) is likely to be permanent. The suspicious questioner is right. The convert will relapse. But that need not be the end of the story. ' That stumble ' at the beginning of the race may prove to be ' Marathon won '.

In these two poems Taliessin has been shown principally as giving (though also, in some degree, receiving) a Beatrician experience. In the next, *The Sister of Percivale*, he receives more fully ; he meets the Beatrice *par excellence* of his whole life. This is the lady Blanchefleur, sister of Percivale and Lamorack. Two things need to be known about her. In the first place she is called Dindrane at one time and Blanchefleur at another. This, I think, is unfortunate and I believe it came about solely because Williams while writing *Taliessin* had forgotten that her name Dindrane occurs in *The High History of the Holy Grail*. In Malory she is known simply as 'Percivale's sister', and Williams gave her the name Blanchefleur.[1] Later, on re-reading *The High History*, he rediscovered her true name, liked it too well to let it go, and adopted it with the explanation (given in *The Calling*) that Dindrane was her baptismal name and Blanchefleur her name 'in religion'. The second and much more important thing about her is that she 'bled a dish full of blood' (Malory, xvii. xi.) to save a sick lady's life and died herself as a result. She is therefore the extreme instance in the poem of 'Exchange' or 'Substitution'.

This is perhaps the most difficult poem in the whole cycle and I am far from claiming that I have mastered it. All I can do is to begin with what is easiest and then go to what is next in hardness and so on till I find I can get no further. In its plainest sense the 'argument' is that Taliessin sees Blanchefleur newly brought to court with her two brothers and is, in a certain fashion, enamoured of her—I say, 'in a certain fashion' because this is a meeting of two unicorns, two celibates between whom nothing but 'intellectual nuptials' are at any stage in question. Let us now go up the second step in our stair of difficulties. Before Blanchefleur enters the courtyard Taliessin has been watching a slave girl (not the girl of the two previous poems) drawing water from the castle well. In her also he has seen the celestial light; of her also he has, if we must use the word, been enamoured. The Beatrician quality of the lady does not in the least 'kill' the Beatrician quality of the barbarian slave. Taliessin is living on that rung of the Platonic ladder whence the soul sees the beauty in all beautiful bodies to be one. Hence, as Williams says in one of the manuscript notes, he sees the slave and the lady as twins; 'Blanchefleur cannot be perfect to understanding without the slave'. This unity between the two

[1] For its origin, see p. 63.

is worked out by an extraordinary unity in diversity between two very different sensuous experiences which the poet establishes at the very moment of Blanchefleur's arrival. The slave's bucket comes up dripping from the well and she lifts it—her arm straight and taut balancing the line of her straight spine. At the same moment comes the announcement of Blanchefleur's party at the gate—

> A trumpet's sound from the gate leaped level with the arm,
> round with breath as that with flesh, to a plan
> blown as that bone-patterned, bound each to a point.

The level continuity of the trumpet blast, made out of something so essentially warm and flexible as air from rounded lips and the rounded straightness of the arm, are both instances of that union between the geometrical and the vital which Williams so often expresses, both fit objects for 'Euclidean love'. Now a further step. The blazon of Percivale's house, and therefore of Blanchefleur's, is a star, as we have learned in earlier poems. And the slave's back is scarred—whether 'from whip or sword' we do not know. Taliessin has watched her at the well until that scar ('the mark flickered white in the light') has led him over 'the curved horizon' of her back into the contemplation of that same 'organic body' which he contemplated in Byzantium —'Jura, Alp, Elburz, Gaul to Caucasia'. That is why, recognizing the unity between the slave and the lady, we can say 'The stress of the scar ran level with the star of Percivale'. The difference, to be sure, is quite as important as the unity. The scar symbolizes all the violence and suffering by which alone barbarian souls can be brought, against their will, into the confines of the City in order that, at a later stage they may, by their will, remain there. The star symbolizes the whole heraldic pattern which the City has for those who are native there, for whom law has been sublimated into honour, service into courtesy, discipline into dance. Blanchefleur and the slave are two as well as one. In the slave we see the back of something which in Blanchefleur reveals its face. Poetically this is driven home by

the fact that we attend almost exclusively to the slave's back—
the scarred shoulder, the 'smooth slopes', the spine ; but
turning, Taliessin saw ' the rare *face* of Blanchefleur '. Perhaps
that is what Blanchefleur is—the slave *turned round* : in older
language, converted. And yet, by a further subtlety, Blanchefleur herself, Blanchefleur's face, is the back of something else.
Substitution which shows its heavenly face in heaven can show
little more than its scarred back in this world ; as God allowed
Moses on the mountain to see His ' back parts ' And so

> the face of Blanchefleur was the grace of the Back in the Mount.

So far I think I understand. But all round this illuminated
area there rolls and pulsates a mass of meanings that escape me.
Williams himself wrote for me as a headline to p. 53 this sentence : ' The perfect union of sensuality and substance is seen for
a moment.' It is plain that the whole poem records the momentary vision of a unity which is more often invisible ; but
the terms sensuality and substance, borrowed from Lady Julian's
Revelations of Divine Love, do not help me very much since I
know neither what Lady Julian meant by them nor what Williams understood her to have meant. *Sensuality* in Middle English normally means ' the sensitive soul ' which we share with
animals, as distinct both from the ' vegetable soul ' which we
share with plants and the ' rational soul ' which we share with
angels : that is, it means the life of the senses. (What we call
' sensuality ' is in Middle English called ' luxury ' or ' gluttony '.)
Williams was not a Middle English scholar and we cannot
assume at the outset that he fully understood Lady Julian's use
of the word : but he certainly understood that *sensuality* in her
language is not a term of disapproval. He found the key to her
meaning (as another of his notes tells me) in the passage where
she says that the City is built at the meeting place of Sensuality
and Substance—at that very border line where the supersensible
joins the sensible, where incarnation or embodiment occurs,
where the Word (in some degree or on some level) becomes flesh.
The poem we are considering is filled with imagery which

suggests that we are between two worlds. The very first words in it are ' the horizon '—though I do not understand why this horizon should be located ' at the back of Gaul. The image of an ' horizon ' (a hard, straight line which at once unites and separates heaven and earth)[1] is repeated in the level top of the wall on which Taliessin is lying. He is also, significantly, ' between ' Arthur's hall and the horizon which are for a second united by a flash of lightning, just as the sensuous and substantial worlds are momentarily united in the Beatrician experience. The slave's back as she stoops makes ' a curved horizon ' beyond which Taliessin sees her ' substantial ' (supersensuous) nature, and ' the horizon in her eyes was breaking with distant Byzantium '. The shape of the hall is cut out against the western sky and thus makes a kind of horizon between Camelot and Broceliande. The bucket coming out of the well is visualized in the line, ' A round plane of water rose shining in the sun.' The image is so ' mature with pure fact ' that it can be enjoyed fully for its own sake : but the writer must have noticed and intended us to notice that ' a round plane ' shining in the sky's light is an exact description of what every horizon contains. But there is still something more in the poem which I have not understood.

In these three pieces we have been shown instances of those acts of courtesy and exchange out of which the king's poet's ' household ' or ' company ' arose. In *The Founding of the Company* we get a fuller account of its character. The ' company ' is an extension of the ' household '—an overflow, or reproduction, into Logres generally of the life lived in Taliessin's own house among his slaves, retainers, and squires. It is something subtly less than a religious order. It has not a rule, only ' a certain pointing ' : it has no name, no formal admission. It is also, I suspect, the most autobiographical element in the cycle. Something like the Company probably came into existence wherever

[1] It may be helpful to remember that Williams once said 'The chief fact about a wood is that in it you have no horizon.' Hence Broceliande is very exactly the *apeiron*.

Williams had lived and worked. In it the whole organic body is represented ; ' rose lordly Caucasia ' in its ' strong base of maids, porters, mechanics ', its ' glowing face ' in Dindrane, its brain in ' the King's college and council '. There are three degrees of membership, but they are separable only by an abstraction (' for convenience of naming ') and all share ' the gay science '. In the lowest degree are those who live ' by a frankness of honourable exchange ' on the social and economic level ; those, in fact, who willingly accept and honourably and happily maintain that complex system of exchanged services on which society depends. There is nothing to distinguish them from people outside the company except the fact that they do consciously and joyously, and therefore excellently, what everyone save parasites has to do in some fashion. From one point of view they are merely good slaves, good soldiers, good clergy, good counsellors and the like. But their goodness in each vocation springs from the fact that they have taken into their hearts the doctrine of Exchange, have made ' singular and mutual confession ' of ' the mansion and session of each in each '. As a result there is, inside the company, no real slavery or real superiority. Slavery there becomes freedom and dominion becomes service. As willed necessity is freedom, so willed hierarchy becomes equality : that is why in the *Crowning* we read

> hierarchic, republican, the glory of Logres.

That glory Logres has failed to capture, but it is achieved in secret by the Company, the ' remnant '. In the second degree are those members of the Company who practise ' Substitution ' as Williams defined it in *He Came Down from Heaven* and illustrated it in *Descent into Hell* : silently, secretly, ' wary of much chatter ', with a certain shyness and yet, in the last resort, ' neither ashamed of taking nor chary of giving '.

The third and highest degree is harder to understand, at least for me. The difficulty is probably not a literary one. An old saint, being asked whether it is easy or hard to love God, replied :

'It is easy *to those who do it.*' This highest degree is, I expect, easy to understand for those who have achieved it. In it the doctrine of Substitution which those of the second degree enact individually, substituting themselves one for one in pairs, is grasped in its totality. They experience, above and beyond particular substitutions, that total reciprocity or co-inherence which first exists in the Blessed Trinity and descends thence into Man who was made in the image of the Trinity and is lost in Man by the Fall and restored to Man by 'the one adored substitution' of Christ. What the Co-inherence means is best seen in the instance of the Blessed Virgin. Christ is born (and borne) of her : she is born (and borne) of Christ. So in humanity as a whole there is not merely an interchange of symmetrical relations (as when, A being the brother of B, B is also the brother of A) but of those unsymmetrical relations which seem incompatible on the level of 'rational virtue'. Each is mother and child, confessor and penitent, teacher and pupil, lord and slave to the other. Each is his neighbour's priest—and victim. Each, if you fix your eyes on him, becomes the exclusive end for whom all the other exist—

> there men
> were known, each alone and none alone
> bearing and borne.

And the archtype of this is the inexpressible co-inherence of the Three Persons in one God. Therefore when Taliessin once saw the land of the Trinity ('from a high deck among tossing seas Beyond Broceliande') he saw

> a deep, strange island of granite growth
> thrice charged with massive light in change,
> clear and golden-cream and rose tinctured,
> each in turn the Holder and the Held—as the eyes
> of the watcher altered and faltered and again saw
> the primal Nature revealed as a law to the creature.

Notice here how symbol within symbol breaks out from the almost crushed (but for that very reason arch-active) imagina-

tion.   As the Three Persons (to our eyes) ' alter and falter ' each
from Holder to Held, so the island alters from light caught in
massive granite to granite charged with massive light.

But the most important passage of this poem is still to come.
In what sense is this company Taliessin's ?   To ask this is to ask
what leadership or lordship can properly mean among redeemed
souls, and how (since such pre-eminences are unavoidable) they
can be exercised without disobeying the words ' Be not called
Rabbi '.   Williams's answer, to anyone who had it from his own
lips and his own life, is as lucid as the sun and (I think) of the
deepest moment.   Yet I can find hardly any words of my own
to express it.   Dinadan, the knight of holy mockery, meeting
Taliessin in the king's rose-garden on All Fools' Day, salutes him
as the Master of the Company.

> 'Well encountered, lieutenant
> (they call you) of God's new grace in the streets of Camelot.'

Taliessin disclaims the title.   To call himself a Master ?—it is a
horrible thing, it is the beginning of the road to P'o-Lu.   But
Dinadan replies in effect that the title, if rightly accepted, is not
so much a terror as a celestial joke ; if truly understood it brings
merry humility to the wearer.   Under no pretext of false
humility is a fact ever to be rejected ; and it is a fact that Taliessin
is a catcher of souls.   But then

> ' Catch as catch can—but the higher caught in the lower,
> the lower in the higher ; any buyer of souls
> is bought himself by his purchase ; take the lieutenancy
> for the sake of the shyness the excellent absurdity holds.'

The absurdity lies in the fact that every one of God's lieutenants
is, in the last resort, wholly superfluous.   God needs none of
them ; ' of these stones ' He can raise up prophets, doctors,
priests, poets, philosophers, guides.   Taliessin's cavalry charge
turned the day at Mount Badon : but it was his men, not he,
who did most of the killing.   They needed him only as a figure-
head ; any other figure-head, had God so willed, would have

done as well. And now Taliessin, with a superficial ruefulness in his smile and a delight far deeper than the ruefulness, recognizes this. He is unnecessary to Dindrane, to Logres, to the Company, even to poetry : nay, poetry itself is unnecessary.

Many writers have in a satiric spirit unmasked human grandeur, delighting to show us that the king, stripped of robes and ceremony, is but clay like other men and that (says Bacon) ' the masks, and mummeries and triumphs of the world ' show more ' stately and daintily ' by the candlelight of illusion than by the ' naked and open ' light of truth. Any sixteenth-century writer —Shakespeare, Erasmus, Montaigne—can roll you out reams of such moralizing, almost in his sleep. Williams's view is different. He accepts all they say. He finds it so obvious as to be hardly worth saying. *Of course* the whole thing is a kind of make believe or fancy-dress ball. Not only official greatness, as of kings or judges, but what we call real greatness, the greatness of Shakespeare, Erasmus, and Montaigne, is, from a certain point of view, illusory. What then ? What but to thank God for the ' excellent absurdity ' which enables us, if it so happen, to play great parts without pride and little ones without dejection, rejecting nothing through that false modesty which is only another form of pride, and never, when we occupy for a moment the centre of the stage, forgetting that the play would have gone off just as well without us—

> such a delicate smile
> such joyous and high-restrained obeisance of laughter
> ordains through all degrees an equality of being.

This is the spirit which ought to govern even the smallest and most temporary assumptions of the higher place ; whenever we forgive or permit or teach we should be aware of the ' excellent absurdity ' but none the less step obediently into our position, assured that if we are some day to come where saints cast down their golden crowns we must here be content both to assume for ourselves and to honour in others crowns of paper and tinsel, most worthy of tender laughter but not of hostile contempt.

> If an image lacks, since God backs all,
> be the image, a needless image of peace
> to those in peace.

The exact chronological position of *Taliessin in the Rose Garden* is hard to determine, but it must be placed before Dindrane's entry into religion. It is the one poem in the cycle which has Guinevere the queen for its main subject, thus defining one more of the elements of failure in Logres. On a day so calm that terrestrial Nature for a moment approximates to the tranquillity of Nature's archtype in the sphere of Venus, and only the ' infinite and infinitesimal trembling of the roses' still reminds us by its delicate disquietude that the energy of Broceliande ' seethes in Logres ', Taliessin, walking and composing, in the garden, looks up and sees Guinevere at the end of the ' level spinal path ' —spinal because the garden is one more image of the organic body. And he sees her as she truly is ; sees both what she was intended to be and what she has become ; sees in the fall of Guinevere the Fall of Man and sees also the cosmic significance of Woman.

It is because he is a unicorn that Taliessin sees all this. He, who has enjoyed no woman in the flesh, has a clearer vision of womanhood than the satisfied lovers. Even of those whose abstinence is involuntary, like Palomides, it may be true that they ' study ' the beloved more than their successful rivals ; and conversely, even the dedicated virgins and catchers of souls like Taliessin find in the cup of their vocation one little drop of that bitterness which is almost all that Palomides tastes : but they do not resent it. This especial clarity of vision in unconsummated love does not mean that fruition (the principle of Touch) reports falsely of the beloved while contemplation (the principle of Eyes) reports truly. Both report truly and both report the same. The difference is that—

> flesh knows what spirit knows
> but spirit knows it knows.

And Taliessin's spirit is ' Druid-born and Byzantium-trained '. What he has learned at Byzantium of the nature of Man is here expressed by the myth of the twelve 'Houses' of the Zodiac. The Acts of Identity issuing from the Emperor split themselves up into this multiplicity, are (for our sakes) thus made many in order

that each mind
in the Empire may find its own kind of entry.

In other words, as St. Paul said, there is a diversity of operations. Different men have different talents, privileges, and obligations. The function of Taliessin is to see—'Aquarius for me opened the principle of eyes'. In Aquarius, the House of Sight, he sees all the other Houses. That is the fashion in which it contains all the rest, as each of them, in some different fashion, contains it : 'All coalesced in each.' As long as Gemini, the House of the operative hands, or Scorpio, the House of generation, or Libra, the House of earth, of the body, of Caucasia, remain in their obedience, every one of them is an 'entry' into the total empire.

In this zodiacal vision Taliessin has seen the true significance of Woman.

I saw how the City
was based, faced fair to the Emperor as the queen to the king,
slaves to lords, and all Caucasia to Carbonek.

Whether consciously or not Williams is here recalling the Greek doctrine that Form is masculine and Matter feminine. This is not very easily translated into terms which a modern reader will understand : but in so far as we still think of the sun as a father and speak of 'Mother Earth' it is not irrecoverable. The earth is full of potential life ; the sun draws it out and makes it actual. So likewise the material of anything, the wood or clay, is full of possibility : the imposition of form makes it into a table or a chair, a statue or a cup. In generation itself the flow of potential life from the female is similarly arrested, determined, actualized by the male seed. In each soul the tide of emotional possibility—the psychic energy—is 'enformed', turned into this or that determinate attitude, by the will and intelligence. 'Slaves to lords' will not seem surprising if we remember that

the power to work in any community becomes actual only when
it is determined to this or that operation by someone's direction.
The whole City, the Divine Order, is a marriage between the
will of the Emperor and the response to that will in His creatures.
Caucasia itself, the body, the world of the senses, is feminine in
relation to Carbonek, the Spirit; for sanctity orders and uses
all the body's energies.

Had all gone well in Logres, Guinevere would have summed
up in herself and exhibited to perfection the element of matter,
of the feminine, of the sensuous, and Arthur would have done
the same for form, for the masculine, for intelligence. Their
marriage would have been the holy wedding of Sun and Earth,
as every true marriage is. Guinevere would have been

> the sensuous mode, the consummate earth of Logres,
> the wife of Arthur, the queen of the Kingdom.

She would have been able to do what Taliessin vainly asks her
to do at the end of this poem when he says

> Let the queen's majesty, the feminine headship of Logres,
> deign to exhibit the glory to the women of Logres;
> each to one vision, but the queen for all.
> Bring to a flash of seeing the women in the world's base.

The last line is difficult but its meaning will become clearer if we
look at the penultimate stanza of *The Departure of Merlin* where
it is repeated. We are there told that Nimue, terrestrial Nature

> brings all natural becoming to her shape of immortal being
> as to a flash of seeing the women in the world's base.

Nimue, in obedience to her lord the Third Heaven, brings the
potentialities of Earth to perfection; just as she also brings ' to
a flash of seeing '—makes suddenly visible to our senses—the
ultimate femininity of the created universe. In the soft fertile
earth of the ploughed fields, in the waters of sea and river, in
shadows and darkness, in the clouds that make sunlight visible
while receiving visibility from it, in all that receives, responds,
brings forth and is enformed, but most of all in a beautiful and
wise woman discerned in a flash of Beatrician seeing, Nature

sets before us for our delight the unfathomable feminine principle which would otherwise lie invisible at the very roots of Broceliande, ' the world's base '. Guinevere, had she risen to her vocation, would have done likewise. She would have been a living and speaking exposition of the innocent body, the right energy, the fruitful earth.

Instead of being such an exposition Guinevere has become one of the agents through which Logres will fall and the shores of Britain lie again defenceless to the ' pirate beaks ' of heathen invaders. Taliessin sees this magically mirrored in the ruby on the queen's ring : this, and much more. The redness of the ruby itself is mingled with the reflected redness of the roses among which she is walking. These, as he looks, become the blood-redness of the wars which will follow the fall of Arthur— the ' moon of blood letting '. Yet in the very heart of that war, though also encircling that war, the stone, which is a sacred stone, still seems to shake with the trembling of the roses, and all these reds merge into the martyred blood of the Grail King, Pelles, bleeding at Carbonek from the Dolorous Blow—

So rich was the ring and by Merlin royally runed.

In the stone Taliessin is seeing both the Fall and the Redemption. In the state of innocence all the Houses of the Zodiac are ' co-inherent ' : each is in all ; whichever you go into, you will find you are at the centre. But since the Fall, instead of Co-inherence there is Incoherence. Aquarius is bloodshot : the Twins tear each other : the Scorpion ' in its privy place ' stings, bringing into action ' the anger of the laden tail '. That ' danger ' in it which had been in the Emperor's mind an unrealized contingency becomes for the children of Adam, and especially for Guinevere, an actuality. We see

The Empire dark with the incoherence of the houses

From this confusion

the way of return
climbed beside the timed and falling blood.

The poet is thinking, of course, about the blood sacrifice of

149

Calvary : but that blood sacrifice is imaged on various lower levels and it is these images which are chiefly presented to us. King Pelles bleeding at Carbonek is the most obvious of them. ' Jupiter's red-pierced planet' which hangs over Carbonek is harder. Williams assumes that the huge reddish spot which astronomers observe on the surface of Jupiter is a wound and the redness is that of blood. Jupiter, the planet of Kingship, thus wounded, becomes, like the wounded King Pelles, another ectype of the Divine King wounded on Calvary. And finally we have one of those physiological symbols which will seem grotesque to many readers but which spring inevitably from the poet's whole view of the body and are meant with all seriousness. The menstrual flow in women presents certain problems on the scientific level in so far as it is not really quite paralleled by what seem at first to be the parallel phenomena in the females of other species. Williams sees it as a ' covenant in the flesh '. By it all women *naturally* share in the great sacrifice. That, indeed, is why they are excluded from the priesthood ; excluded from the office because they thus share mystically in the role of the Victim ;

> Well are women warned from serving the altar
> who, by the nature of their creature, from Caucasia to Carbonek,
> share with the Sacrifice the victimization of blood.

Of course only converted women know that they do so and can will their necessity, for

> Flesh tells what spirit tells
> (but spirit knows it tells). Women's travel
> holds in the natural the image of the supernatural.

All this Taliessin thinks while he watches Guinevere in the rose garden. No words pass between them till the very end of the poem : then, as they meet, the queen raises her eyebrows and says to the silent poet

> with the little scorn that becomes a queen of Logres
> ' Has my lord dallied with poetry among the roses ? '

It becomes a great queen, this raillery : that is, it would become her if she were true lady, if this playful mockery were the bloom or sparkle on the surface of a true wealth of courtesy and wisdom. Had she been good she need not, on this occasion, have been graver.

Two spiritual maxims were constantly present to the mind of Charles Williams : ' This also is Thou ' and ' Neither is this Thou '. Holding the first we see that every created thing is, in its degree, an image of God, and the ordinate and faithful appreciation of that thing a clue which, truly followed, will lead back to Him. Holding the second we see that every created thing, the highest devotion to moral duty, the purest conjugal love, the saint and the seraph, is no more than an image, that every one of them, followed for its own sake and isolated from its source, becomes an idol whose service is damnation. The first maxim is the formula of the Romantic Way, the ' affirmation of images ' : the second is that of the Ascetic Way, the ' rejection of images '. Every soul must in some sense follow both. The Ascetic must honour marriage and poetry and wine and the face of nature even while he rejects them ; the Romantic must remember even in his Beatrician moment ' Neither is this Thou '. But souls are none the less called to travel principally the one way or the other, and in the next poem (*The Departure of Dindrane*) this distinction of vocations is set before us. Dindrane and Taliessin, spiritually wedded, not despite the difference of their vocations but because of it, part for ever, she to follow the ascetic way in the convent of Almesbury and he to continue the romantic way at Camelot and Caerleon.

The poem is woven of two strands. The one concerns Taliessin and Dindrane, riding together at the head of their little cavalcade through the incessant rain to a certain point on the road outside Camelot where they bid one another good-bye. The coinherence of their opposite vocations is expressed in their parting words. Dindrane, on the way of rejection, says to the poet ' I will affirm, my beloved, all that I should.' He, on the way of affirmation, replies ' I will reject all that I should.' It should be noticed that there is a complete absence of the human pathos with which almost any other writer would have treated this moment of separation. There may have been conflict in the soul of each at some earlier stage; we are not shown that stage. In each of them now the natural passion is not so much 'mortified,' as set on fire, by the spiritual : their human love survives in their fully and rapturously accepted vocations as red-hot coal survives in fire ; nay, it *is* now vocation as the red coal *is* the fire. Hence Taliessin

> turned his horse aside : he *burned* on the household
> crying, ' All, with the Princess to Almesbury ',
> and again to me at Camelot. Dindrane, farewell !

And as for Dindrane,

> the shell of her body
> yearned along the road to the cell of vocation.

The other strand concerns a slave woman who, as part of her duty in Taliessin's household, is riding to Almesbury with Dindrane. It will be noticed that Dindrane (or Blanchefleur) has once already been accompanied and balanced by a slave in *The Sister of Percivale*. For the slave and the princess, the worker and the contemplative, are coinherent and neither can be fully understood without the other. Hence, in the present poem, we see Dindrane and Taliessin through the slave's eyes.

The girl has a problem of her own to solve. In Logres, as in ancient Israel, slavery lasted only for seven years. At the end of that time you had your choice of three things. You could be sent home to your own country. You could stay in Logres as a free citizen, and be given a start in life (' for a woman a dowry for a man a farm '). Or thirdly, you could freely, but irrevocably, choose to remain a servant in the house you already belonged to. And for this slave girl the time has almost come ; she must make her choice next week.

The catch about the third alternative is, obviously, the irrevocability. One might so easily regret it. And then her master Taliessin has this regrettable characteristic, that

the king's poet
lightened no heart except when the heart heightened,
and what heightening was sure to endure such doom ?

It is, in fact, with the service of a beloved human master as it is with the service of the Master Himself. Dryness will come in the one service as in the other. And it seems to be just at those moments of dryness, when the Master's help is most needed, that the Master gives no help at all. At other moments, indeed, favour comes without asking and in full measure : but those seem (to human frailty) to be the moments when you could almost have done without it : everything was already so well.

Thus the girl puzzles over her problem, sitting her stationary horse in the rain. Then the doors open. Dindrane comes out. The girl likes Dindrane. She suddenly sees that Dindrane has been dealing with the very same problem. She also, in resolving to take the veil, has accepted servitude. Her resolve is shining bright on her face

and all circumstance of bondage blessed in her body . . .
The jointed and linked fetters were the jointed bones,
manacles of energy were manipulations of power.

Then, as Dindrane and Taliessin descend the steps, and the escort salute them, the slave sees in that moment of ceremonial rigidity how 'servitude and freedom were one and interchangeable'. Or rather, the only difference is that while both obey, servitude obeys an 'imaged' and freedom an 'unimaged' law. But now the party is moving off.

Still the girl keeps her eyes fixed on the two figures of the Poet and the Princess at the head of the column, hooded and cloaked against the rain, and looking—they and their horses— like two centaurs. And still she is trying to choose. Can she, even she, ever become a being like those two ? She cannot see herself so perfected : and rightly cannot see. That sight, if it is ever to come, will be for other eyes, for her child, her lover, for God Himself. And on each side of them the hazel bushes go past—the 'uncut' hazels of wildness and freedom, the apparent opposite of the straight hard road and of all straight hard things which are made out of cut hazels. Yet the nuts of the uncut hazels fall on to the disciplined road.

But has she really any choice? Is this hesitation between alternatives anything more than an imperfection? For the full-grown soul the best must be visible and inevitable. All at once there sounds in the slave's ears a voice from the sphere of Venus, the third heaven—'Fixed is the full'. The climax of Nimue (Nature) is 'tranquil in Venus'. All this variation, this hithering and thithering of the compass needle, is preparatory and incomplete. True freedom is not to be found there. The truly free choice of the soul expresses her deepest nature and is in that sense necessary, could not be otherwise—' the freedom of the rose-tree is the rose'. The slave girl during her apparent indecision has really been discovering what she had already decided and what, being a pure soul, she could not but have decided. Hence, seven days later, she comes before the king's bailiff and swears to remain in the household of Taliessin.

The obscurity of the words in which she does so masks what I take to be a piece of good psychology. All through that wet ride her whole attention has been fixed on Taliessin and Dindrane. The very jingling of their bits as they rode has beaten its tune into her brain till it has become the symbol of the challenge she was accepting and the standard against which she has had to measure herself. Now at last she is 'quits with those two jingling bits'. She has won her victory, without any word or sign from her master to help her; indeed no word or sign could have helped her unless she had been ripe enough in spirit to make the choice without them. That is the explanation of the apparently cruel paradox that ' the King's poet lightened no heart except when the heart heightened '. The Father can be well pleased in that Son only who adheres to the Father when apparently forsaken. The fullest grace can be received by those only who continue to obey during the dryness in which all grace seems to be withheld. The same is true, in degree, of every human master—

> They only can do it with my lord who can do it without him,
> and I know he will have about him only those.

In all the poems which deal with Taliessin's ' Household ' we have seen various stages in the progress of his ' slaves ' from barbarism to Christian ripeness. In *The Queen's Servant* we see the consummation of this process. This difficult and daring poem is best understood if we remember, firstly, St. Paul's longing to be rid of the mortal body not in order that he may be unclothed but that he may be clothed anew (2 Cor. v. 4) and, secondly, that place in the *Purgatorio* where Virgil having brought Dante to the earthly Paradise sets him free from all tutelage and makes him henceforth emperor and pontiff over himself. We are shown, in fact, the moment at which a soul is redeemed into the glorious liberty of the children of God. Treating the poem allegorically you might say that Taliessin is here a type of Christ : but it is not an allegory and we had better say that Christ in Taliessin is operative—as in all our guides and teachers.

Sir Kay sends to Taliessin directing him to supply from his household a maid for the queen's service ; a post, this, for a free woman not a slave. In obeying this order Taliessin is therefore emancipating a slave ; the ceremonial blow which he strikes her at the end of the poem is borrowed from the ceremony of emancipation in Roman law. But both the slave and the poet know that he is also emancipating her in a far deeper sense : just as he (or Christ in him) had originally ' bought ' her in a deeper sense. Hence, though she has, from one point of view, deserved or earned her freedom, she has earned it only ' with his gold '. Since it is grace that enables us to work, our works can never balance our accounts with God. She is still ' his purchase '. It is in Caucasia he bought her : she was mere ' flesh ' or ' nature ' before she was redeemed. For her the change has been absolute : she has no notion how closely that same Caucasia mirrors the supernature or arch-nature into which she is now entering. Taliessin, wandering in Caucasia has seen the roses, the golden-fleeced lambs, and the ' flurry of snow . . . bright as a sudden irrepressible smile '. But she, the native of Caucasia, has never seen them, for though flesh (in a sense) ' knows what spirit knows ', only ' spirit knows it knows '. Only when we look back from supernature do we see what nature really meant.

To understand this intellectually is an arduous work of metaphysics—you must see the map in Merlin's books or that ' one small title ' from the Emperor's own atlas which a very few sages have been allowed to look at. But there is a much shorter, though in some respects, a harder, way. The discovery can be lived. The command to live it is expressed in the single word ' unclothe '. To pass into the glorious liberty and so to experience the true relations of Nature and Supernature (' Arch-nature ' Williams always preferred to call it) we must become naked ; we must even become ' nothing '. God gives His gifts where He finds the vessel empty enough to receive them. Then we shall know ' the Rite that invokes Sarras '.

The slave obeys. In her naked body, Caucasia's gift to her, Taliessin sees what she cannot see. Through these curves shines the straightness of Byzantium ; and something more. As well as Byzantium (the throne of God in His ' imperial ' or Providential aspect) there is Sarras, the far western land of the Co-inherent Trinity where dwell the mysteries of immanence and incarnation, deeper and sweeter than those of transcendence :—

> through the rondures, eyes quick as clear
> see, small but very certain, Byzantium,
> or even, in a hope, the beyond-sea meadows
> that, as in a trope, Caucasia shadows.

For Caucasia, had we but eyes to see it, has all along ' shadowed ' Sarras, been like Arch-nature in its very unlikeness, as a ' trope ' or metaphor in poetry is unlike, yet eminently like, the thing it symbolizes. The death of the body prepares for the resurrection —of the body.

The nakedness, the humiliation, the ' nothing ' which the slave has become, are only preparatory to re-clothing and glory and positive reality. At Taliessin's bidding she stretches out her hands : instantly they are filled with roses. Again and again she repeats the act, flinging at the poet's feet roses and still more roses till ' the whole room was shaded crimson from them '. A moment later it is filled with the bleating of lambs,

> Visibly forming, there fell on the heaped roses
> tangles and curds of golden wool ; the air
> was moted gold in the rose-tinctured chamber.

Of golden wool and crimson rose Taliessin magically makes her garment. Clothed in this glory, she is set free and dismissed with the words ' Be as Ourself in Logres'.

This rich poem is the last of those which are specially concerned with that vocation which Taliessin had been promised in *The Calling* when Merlin said

It may be that this gathering of souls, that the king's poet's household shall follow in Logres and Britain the spiritual roads.

After this we return to the main action which is now hastening towards its catastrophe. In Williams, as in Malory, the opening of the adventures of the Grail strikes a double note. ' When this rich thing goeth about the Round Table shall be destroyed ' —but also redeemed. Judgement is at hand, promise of judgement and threat of judgement. Some are going to find Sarras : others will be involved in the whole ruin whereby Logres sinks into mere Britain. It is the same sort of ambivalence which Christians have been taught to recognize in the season of Advent.

V

The Grail and the Morte

THE first poem in this section, *The Son of Lancelot*, is the
turning-point of the whole cycle ; and the turning-point of
this poem is the lines on page 60—

> The Emperor in Byzantium nodded to the exarchs ;
> it was night still when the army began to move,
> embarking disembarking, before dawn Asia
> awoke to hear the songs, the shouts, the wheels
> of the furnished lorries rolling on the roads to the east.

The army has marched. It is going to ' renew the allegiance of
Caucasia ' now in the hands of the Mohammedan or the Manichaean. That is, it is going to restore the doctrine of the
Incarnation, to proclaim again the redemption of the flesh. The
tide, in fact, has turned, and it has turned because Galahad has
that very hour been born at Carbonek, Galahad the type of Christ
yet son of Lancelot, as Christ Himself was the son of Adam,
Lancelot's only true glory yet also his supreme shame, the fruit
of Lancelot yet also the judgement upon him.

It is important at this point to remember the bare bones of
the story. Lancelot, coming to the castle of Case near Carbonek, has been deceived by the magic of Brisen so that Elayne
the daughter of Pelles looks to him like Guinevere. So deceived
he lies with her. Waking next morning, now freed from the
enchantment, he sees the stranger in his bed and realizes that he
has committed the unforgivable sin of the medieval lover—
infidelity to his mistress. He is hardly restrained from killing
Elayne. The matter comes to the queen's ears and she dismisses
Lancelot in jealous rage. He becomes mad and lives for many
months as a wild man in the woods.

Williams has given the madness of Lancelot a deeper significance. Carbonek, where Lancelot found Elayne, lies as we know

' beyond a certain part of Broceliande '. To have reached
Carbonek, therefore, he must have been in the ' sea-wood '.
And it is a place where Taliessin feared

> lest dread or desolation wrecked his mind
> So that he fell from his kind,

a place where ' Circe's son ' (shape-changing Comus)

> sings to the truants of towns
> in a forest of nightingales.
> The beast ran in the wood
> that had lost the man's mind.

When Lancelot leaped from the window of Elayne's bedroom
and ran into that wood he became something worse than a mad-
man ; he suffered the change which old authors call Lycanthropy
and turned into a wolf—' he grew Backward all summer, laired
in the heavy wood '. For Broceliande is the way to sub-normal
as well as to supra-normal states of being. It leads down to the
world of D. H. Lawrence as well as up to the world of Blake :
the soul that enters it unpurified will be likely to ' grow backward '. Lancelot is the flower of earthly chivalry but he is
flawed. The animal in him has, all along, lived untamed and
uncorrected inside that chivalry : he has been

> the King's mind's blood
> The lion in the blood roaring through the mouth of creation.

His love for Guinevere which might, by abstaining from the
flesh, have become such a spiritual marriage as Taliessin celebrates
with Dindrane, has taken and obstinately (even, in the *Star of
Percivale*, idolatrously) adhered to a forbidden path, involving

> the raging eyes, the rearing bodies, the red
> Carnivorous violation of intellectual love.

The spiritual lion in him has grown backward into spiritual wolf
and the spiritual wolf worked outward till he is bodily wolf as
well, howling and sniffing about the doors of Carbonek in human
hatred and animal hunger for the child whom Elayne is to bear.
He would devour Galahad.

The figure of the wolfish Lancelot is important because in a work devoted mainly to the glorification of the flesh he is one of Williams's few expressions of the dangers of concupiscence. It is important also because the idea of Wolf, thus introduced, dominates the poem.

Wolves, to a European, mean Winter : hence snow covers the landscape of this poem and by an inevitable association the connexion between the birth of Galahad and the birth of Christ is pressed upon the reader's mind. But Wolves mean, more particularly, the Wolf-month of the old Roman calendar, February. And in February were celebrated the *Lupercalia*. Readers of Shakespeare's *Julius Caesar* will remember that at this festival a chance blow from the sacred thong conferred fertility upon the woman who received it, so that the Wolf-Feast is connected with nativities : not least with the nativity of those twins whom Rhea Silvia bore to Mars and who were suckled by a wolf. On the other hand wolves mean desolation. Wherever men become ' truants of towns ', wherever the City falls back, heathen, war, and wolf press on.

There is thus throughout the poem an amazing counterpoint of ideas : the ' top tune ' or, changing the metaphor, the focus which brings all into unity, is supplied by Merlin. His behaviour is, for me, a little obscured by technicalities of magic, a subject in which Williams was more learned than most of us. I am compelled to accept these as a mere romantic penumbra because of my ignorance ; but I am quite sure that was not how they were written. Williams probably knew all about the ' anatomical body of light ' and the ' illustration ' of the ' grades '. Magic for him ' throws no truck with dreams ' : its instrument is ' the *implacable* hazel '—the straight, cut rod of discipline and measure. The conjuring of Merlin—the thrust of Time, Destiny, History —exhibits that mysterious onward pressure which brings events to pass : mysterious to us, because we are ignorant, but doubtless, in itself, as precise and articulate as a geometrical diagram.

Merlin conjures at Camelot in ' the thin night air of Quinquagesima'—and with that word there blow across the cold fields colder airs from Lent and hunger and contrition. He sees the world in three ' circles '. In the first he sees the shrinking of the Empire, the creeping return of chaos, consequent upon the Dolorous Blow and the whole failure of Logres. Everywhere the watch fires are reflected ' in the packed eyes of forest-emerging wolves '. In the second circle he sees Logres itself, both the good and the evil of it. Taliessin and Bors are still at their posts and Blanchefleur follows her vocation at Almesbury. But the king has surrendered to his egoism, ' dreaming of a red Grail in an ivory Logres '. In the third circle Merlin has risen to where he sees things from the point of view of the third Heavenly sphere, the ' feeling intellect ', the ' climax tranquil in Venus '. From there we see the sublunary world of Nimue in its eternal reality ; seen from there, we remember, the very ' stones of the waste glimmer like summer stars '. In that high place Merlin hears as a single chord the Roman wives, centuries ago, crying at the Lupercalia, the Pope singing Mass on Lateran, and the wolf that had been Lancelot howling from Broceliande at the closed gates of Carbonek. He descends, following that howl.

After that the poem becomes comparatively simple. The story of Galahad's begetting and birth (' The child slid into space, into Brisen's hands ') and Lancelot's lycanthropy is recapitulated. Merlin sets out, passes the guards at Camelot gate, and now becoming himself a huge white wolf gallops across the snow to Carbonek. As he reaches its gates the other were-wolf, Lancelot, leaps at him. But ' the force of the worlds ' is in Merlin and

> nine yards off
> the falling head of Lancelot struck the ground.
> Senseless he lay

Brisen comes to the door and binds the new-born child on Merlin's back. Merlin, still in his animal form, delivers it to Blanchefleur at Almesbury there to be nurtured, and returns laughing, by dawn, to Camelot. And soon after this, in the guest chamber at Carbonek

> Lancelot lay, tended, housed and a man,
> To be by Easter healed and horsed for Logres.

Two more points perhaps require a word of comment. Firstly, we should note the distinction between the wolf-form of Merlin and the wolf-form of Lancelot. For the imagination it is possibly enough that the one should be white and beneficent, the other grey and ravening. But if the intellect wishes to press further, we may point out that Merlin becomes wolf of his own will and Lancelot against his will and beyond his understanding. Lancelot is the beast ' that had lost the man's mind ' : Merlin is the man's mind using and controlling the beast's speed and strength. In the second place, it may be asked why Guinevere in her midnight jealousy and loneliness is called ' the queen's tormented unaesthetic womanhood '. Clearly, her state of evil is being contrasted with the aesthetic evil of the king. Arthur is an aesthete : imagination is the medium through which his egoism corrupts him. Guinevere is not at all an aesthete : she is an angry, mortally wounded woman whose thoughts go round and round the same circular groove. By the words ' unaesthetic womanhood ' I think Williams means to direct our thoughts to something which is really characteristic of the feminine mind— that monopolistic concentration, for good or ill, on the dominant idea, which brings it about that in a woman good states of mind are unweakened and undissipated, or bad states of mind unrelieved, by fancy and speculation and mere drifting. Hence that tenacity both of good and evil, those chemically pure states of devotion or of egoism, which are hardly conceivable in my own sex. The lady in Mr. Eliot's poem who said ' How you digress ' was speaking for all women to all men.

A single poem is all we have to fill the gap of time between Galahad's birth and his arrival, as a young man, at Camelot. Perhaps if Williams had lived other poems would have come in here. Yet the arrangement as it stands is not an unhappy

one, for the single poem *Palomides Before his Christening* is a
poem of prolonged, monotonous stillness : it would be quite
appropriate to imagine it filling fifteen or twenty years.
Here, and here alone, Williams approaches the temper of Mr.
Eliot's later poetry. The dry rock scenery, the artfully prosaic
sentences, the sense of a vast pause, a vacuity, which may be
the prelude either to conversion or despair, all remind us of
the other poet. There is even an echo of Mr. Eliot's manner
in the lines

> The Chi-Ro is only a scratching like other scratchings ;
> But in the turn of the sky the only scratching.

The borrowing seems to me to be ill-judged. No two great
poetic styles are less likely to mix fruitfully than those of Williams
and Mr. Eliot. The passage about skeleton loves which comes
a little earlier is also reminiscent : but the influence here might
also be that of Miss Edith Sitwell's *Metamorphosis*—though I
doubt whether Williams knew her poetry as well as he knew
Mr. Eliot's.

Williams's own note on this poem reads as follows : ' Romantic love and social order have both become blank. All that there
is is hardness and itch and scratchings on the rock. Dinadan
realizes that loss may be a greater possession than having : and
Palomides, incapable of believing believingly, believes unbeliev-
ingly.' All conversion involves death and re-birth ; but sometimes the one, sometimes the other, of these elements is more
noticeably present to the consciousness of the patient. Hence
there are joyous conversions which ' come like hurtless light ' ;
one of them has been described in *The Star of Percivale*. The
flooding in of the new life is so rapturously felt that the death
of the old is (at that moment anyway—there will be painful
stumbles later on) hardly felt as pain. But there are also dark
conversions in which the slow, aching ebb of the old life and
the dryness which it leaves as it ebbs are deeply felt, and the new
life comes with no ' sensible consolation '. Coventry Patmore
has expressed the contrast better, I think, than any other poet.

In the first kind Grace seems only to bid Nature do in a better way what she was doing already. The man to whom this happens is like one who, already walking, hears distant music and then 'his step unchanged, he steps in time'. But in the other kind, the soul, after struggles that seem to have killed it, ' on God's hest almost despairing goes '. Palomides' conversion is an extreme instance of the second kind. It is by way of total humiliation. And even humiliation is of two kinds. Dinadan has almost from the first accepted humiliation with frolic laughter. He is the happy ironist, the Tumbler of Our Lady, the *jongleur de Dieu* : the man who ' gives himself away ' with both hands, delighted at ' the excellent absurdity '. For him therefore the valley of humiliation is green and pleasant as in Bunyan's map. Palomides comes to see, like Dinadan, that one must ' look a fool before everyone '. And like Dinadan he accepts this truth —' Why not look a fool before everyone ? ' But he does not ' believe it believingly '. It is to him mere brute fact. He can submit to the rod but he cannot see the joke. He is the dry convert—until the last moment almost the sulky convert. Theologically he is a most important figure. It concerns us much to know that God accepts even such converts as this : nay, has perhaps even an especial tenderness for them because they have grown ' mature with pure fact ', with the very rock-structure of fact in regions where there are neither flowers nor water. And he comes properly at this place in the cycle. This is another kind of Advent than the coming of the Grail and a necessary pendent to the Grail story.

Palomides has come into the world of dry rock through his struggle with carnal jealousy and thwarted ambition. From the resented humiliation of his first meeting with Iseult he has gone away determined to do some great thing, to ' get his own back ' on the Round Table by doing something that none of them can do. Later on, on his own terms, he will consent to be christened. But first he must put himself in the right. He will catch the Questing Beast. That will make everyone admire him. Their admiration will end the ' gnats ' and ' whirring mosquitoes ' of

thought which torment him, the biting insect-like progeny of
lust and wounded sexual vanity and wounded military vanity—

> They would vanish : the crowd's mass of open mouths,
> the City opening its mouths, would certainly swallow them.

But everything has gone wrong. He has met failure after
failure. The man sinks into himself—' I followed myself away
from the city '—climbs and clambers further and further away
into the world of smooth, polished, waterless rock. At last he
is completely imprisoned in the cave of his own resentment and
concupiscence.

> I sat and scratched.
> Smoke in a greasy thickness rolled round the cave,
> from flames of fierce fancy, flesh-fire-coloured.

Oddly enough—yet we see it happen every day—he prizes his
imprisonment. Though the cave offers nothing but bitter desire,
' the eternal anguish of the skeleton ', his spirit hates the little
current of air which enters from the outer world.

We expect that deliverance from this cave will come in some
spectacular way, that Palomides will do something and we shall
be able to draw a moral. But it is not always like that in real
life. Somehow (only the merciful Emperor knows how) such
moods end : as if they had burned themselves out leaving only
' flimsy ash ' which will burn no longer. Palomides simply
becomes a little frightened and steps out of the cave. But then
' the sky had turned round '.

Nothing remains but the numb, laborious journey over the
rocks, back to Caerleon and Dinadan. There is no ' sensible
consolation ' at all. The Chi-Ro (the two first letters of *Christos*
as we find them sometimes cut in the catacombs) *feel* just like
any other scratched marks. ' Dull, undimensioned I ride at last
to Dinadan.' And even now he has no idea of what Dinadan
really is. He thinks that he is merely *below* the hard Byronic
sort of irony which he (Palomides) would like to have adopted
if the Omnipotence had left him the least chance of doing so.

For Palomides is still only a spiritual infant and understands irony only in its lowest, its ' disillusioned ', form.

The *Coming of Galahad* takes place on the evening of that day on which Palomides was baptized. This day has at once begun the redemption and sealed the fate of Camelot ; Galahad has come to court. He has begun to fulfil the prophecies. He has sat in the Siege Perilous. The water in which he has washed his hands has become phosphorescent, as the beloved, seen in the Beatrician vision ' walks dropping light '. The Grail itself has appeared in hall ; by its grace every one has found on the table the food and drink that he likes best. (This ' liking best ', the act of preferring, is one main theme of the poem.) Now in the evening Galahad is being ceremonially conducted to lie in Arthur's bed—the New Man taking the place of the Old. But we see this ritual only from outside ; there is a vivid image here of the candle-light, seen from without, in window after window of the great staircase as the procession winds up to Arthur's bedchamber. But we, meanwhile, are outside in the cold and unsavoury yard ' among the jakes and latrines ', with Gareth (the prince of Orkney, serving incognito as a house-boy) and Taliessin, and a slave or so. Their conversation forms the main action of the piece.

It turns chiefly on the subject of Preference. To a man of such diverse talents and interests as Williams, a man to whom worship, love, poetry, and philosophy must each have seemed at certain moments to be so infinite that it could hardly be regarded as a part of life, but must be life itself, the problem may have been a pressing one. It would have been easy for him to say that religion must by its very nature over-ride all the others. But that does not carry us very far. For each of these ' Houses ', at least for such a man as he, claims to be ' religion ', even to be Christian religion. Each leads to Byzantium and the Emperor, and each (under Him) claims its own autonomy from all the rest. The practical problem remains unsolved. Poetry no doubt is a way of approaching God : but a poetry directly and consciously subordinated to the ends of edification usually becomes bad poetry. Human love no doubt also is an approach ; but

Williams repeatedly warned young couples not to endeavour to realize this by any over-conscious intention. He thought nothing more ridiculous and disastrous than any attempted subjection of the natural playfulness of Caucasia to some kind of quasi-sacramental gravity.[1] All the different Houses prove true entries to the Empire only on condition of their remaining themselves. You can of course take the Ascetic Way, the way of the rejection of images : the consciously religious life may be so lived as simply to exclude all else. But if you take the Way of Affirmation—what then ? How shall we co-ordinate all the diverse elements ; intellectual, mystical, ecclesiastical, aesthetic, erotic ?

This problem is the real reason why the discussion goes on 'among the jakes and latrines'. Williams's ruthless physiological symbolism leaves nothing out. The fact that the organism can ' reject and elect '—reject its waste products and elect its proper nourishment—is the Caucasian counterpart of the spirit's power to choose and to repent, to cast out what is rejected ; in other words, to prefer. 'Without this alley-way how can man prefer ?'

But the subject of Preference is reached through another. The right preparation (and it is a pleasant one) for reading this poem is to read again the first hundred and sixty-odd lines of Wordsworth's *Prelude*, Book V. It will be remembered that Wordsworth there tells us his dream ; how in a sandy waste he met a mounted Bedouin carrying a stone and a shell, and was given to understand that the stone was ' Euclid's elements ' and the shell was ' something of more worth ' : a shell full of prophetic sound. The Bedouin in fact is carrying Intellect and Poetry. He is going to bury them in order that they may be saved from a flood which is coming upon the Earth, and coming so quickly that Wordsworth, looking over his shoulder sees

> over half the wilderness diffused
> A bed of glittering light,

which is the water already gathering upon him. (Williams

[1] Cf. p. 58.

recalls this image in his line about ' the glittering sterile smile of the sea that pursues '.)

It will easily be imagined what this passage in his great predecessor meant to a poet whose imagination so moved upon the two poles of the geometric and the vital. The shell and the stone become for him Broceliande and Byzantium, Nimue and the Third Heaven, the uncut hazel and the cut hazel, feeling and understanding, or (as Gareth says) ' sound ' and ' measurement.'

Gareth has seen ' among the slaves from the hall's door ' the appearance of the Grail. He asks Taliessin who Galahad is that for him ' the Emperor lifts the Great Ban '. Taliessin replies by quoting from the old Druidical books the distinction between the stone and the shell. This Gareth can understand because he also has read it in ' a book by a Northern poet ' and has himself in a dream watched ' Logres pouring like ocean ' (I suppose, because Logres has now become sterile like the sea) after a girl who fled from it to save ' bright shell, transparent stone '. Well, says Taliessin in effect, that is the answer to your question. To-day the stone has been fitted to the shell in the person of Galahad, the New Man. In him is realized the union which ought to have been realized in Logres as a whole. For as Williams says in one of his notes ' The shell must be fitted to the stone to breed there and burst from it ; this is the finding of Identity ; without it we remain pseudo-romantics.' Taliessin claims to have seen this ' fitting ' achieved in five different Houses ; in the House of Poetry (the Druid Oak), in the life of the flesh (Caucasia), in the intellect (Gaul), in the Church (Lateran or Canterbury) and even in the vision itself (Byzantium). It might be supposed that intellectual Gaul neither needed nor admitted the shell, or that ' gay ' Caucasia neither needed nor admitted the stone. But it is not so : ' *each* house ' is double.

That is the first problem of life : to ' fit ' the stone and the shell in whatever House you occupy, to retain poetic vision in the midst of hard thinking, to study ' precision ' in your highest poetry, to offer even to the *body* of the beloved a ' Euclidean love '. The second problem is suddenly put to Taliessin by a slave girl. We have dealt with the internal economy of each House : but what of the relations *between* the Houses ? She puts it simply by asking Taliessin which food he had *preferred* at that moment when the Grail filled the table with all foods. At first Taliessin suggests that this is not the real problem. ' More choice is within the working than goes before.' The choosing *inside* your own house—the effort, say, to follow the ' theology ' rather than ' the superstitions ' of Romantic Love, if you are a lover—is perhaps more pressing, as it is undoubtedly more neglected, than the problem of choosing your House. Yet the girl's question must be answered.

Here, almost for the first time, Taliessin speaks uncertainly. He says that when all foods were before him he preferred ' what was there '—the first thing that came to hand. Is that the answer ? The preferable House is, for the ripe spirit, always simply the House straight in front of you : the present, the actual, the thing thrown up by seeming chance out of the concrete situation ? Does that mean, asks the girl, that they are really the same ? Can we, in virtue of the maxim *This also is Thou*, regard the apparent differences as superficial or even subjective ? Is Felicity simply one ? Taliessin answers her ' in haste '. Whatever may be the truth, that certainly is not. Felicity not only alters, it ' alters from its centre '. The *differentia* is central : a lifetime of distinguishing would not be enough to mark and adore the utter difference, even the incommensurableness, of our diverse experiences. Because they are so different we must be ' free to taste each alteration ' ; but ' why change till the range twirls ? ' If we enter wholeheartedly the House whose door is presented at any given moment, if we prefer the given, God will do the changing.

But Taliessin admits that he has never seen his way clearly through this question. Whenever he tried to relate any of these five experiences to the others, the shells became empty. The ' Child ' was still-born. Galahad, the holy Child, who could unerringly unite the five Houses by a pentagram, did not come to life. While we are busy trying to measure vital experiences the thing to be measured has vanished. There remains, as the slave reminds him, only the external measurement of harsh moral discipline. (You must stop reading poetry now because it is your duty to do something else.) This is wholesome as far as it goes : perhaps if it is combined with the acceptance of the present House as best—

> if the heart fare
> on what lies ever now on the board, stored
> meats of love, laughter, intelligence and prayer

this answer will do. The slave, brilliantly altering a silly popular expression, replies ' Who knows ?—and who does not care ? '

It is essential throughout this discussion to remember that no one knew better than Williams the orthodox answer, that God and His service must fill the whole life. The question is how that answer is to be interpreted from moment to moment, supposing you do not take the ascetic way and simply say of love *mulier est hominis confusio*, and of poetry ' Demons' wine ', and of philosophy *Down, Reason, down*. All Christendom, almost, assumes that it can be done : but perhaps it seems easy only to shallow minds. If you do not effectively enter *any* of the Houses all will seem plain sailing.

Taliessin at any rate does not give the answer. The answer is Galahad. If you like, the answer is Man—Man in his perfection. In *The Place of·the Lion* Williams had shown us Adam naming (and therefore ruling) the Beasts—the angels who ought to be balanced in his nature but who, loosed from that ' balance and poise ', are monstrous. That, at least, is as much as I can understand. I am baffled by Taliessin's speech to the slave beginning ' O office of all lights ' and also by the passage ' Proofs were, roofs were '. No doubt the general meaning is that the five houses, in each of which the shell had to be fitted to the stone, are in concrete and glorified Man brought back to unity.

> The clerks of the Emperor's house study the redaction
> of categories into identity.

And that would apparently entail the end of the Houses as

we understood them. 'Proofs' (the intellectual House of Gaul) have gone. 'Creeds' (Lateran and Canterbury) have gone. 'Songs' (the poetic House, the Druid Oak) have gone. The two remaining Houses, Caucasia and Byzantium, must therefore be meant by 'Roofs' and 'I': or else 'Roofs' must mean Caucasia ('I what more?' being a parenthesis) and Byzantium alone remains. But why Caucasia should be called 'Roofs' I have no idea.

Williams's own headline for the whole of p. 24 reads 'Taliessin sees the process and triumph of the soul's fruition'. This is presented in the form of an ascent to the Heaven of Heavens, 'the Throne's firmament', through four planetary zones. The first is that of Mercury, the god of theft. I think (but very tentatively) that he means that stage in which the Houses are in crude competition, each anxious to steal the whole glory. Young antinomian decadents hotly demanding that morality should be subjected to the interests of 'Art', or scientists demanding that 'the search for truth' should as a matter of course override justice, mercy, and social order, are still in the zone of Mercury. Venus is the sphere of preference: Love's choice of the Lady, each man's choice of his vocation. It excludes other ladies, other Houses, but with courtesy, recognizing their right to exist. With Jupiter we reach something much subtler. His two moons (Williams seems to have forgotten that he has four) represent two kinds of irony. One is the kind which Lancelot suffered when he begat Galahad at Carbonek. For him the situation was one of what the critics call 'tragic irony': so terrible that it turned him into a beast. The other is 'defeated irony', irony with its sting drawn, accepted by the victim with laughter at its 'excellent absurdity'. On the dramatic plane its great representative is Dinadan: but in another sense its representative is Blanchefleur. It is she who receives into a religious house and nurtures to his perfection that Galahad who was for Lancelot merely a 'taunt'; as in every man the regenerate part can accept the 'taunts' at which his natural man would writhe, and nurture them till each becomes a High Prince. But how this is connected with the problem of the five Houses, or what Saturn represents, I do not know. The poem, for me, ends in riddles.

When a man is studying a difficult work of art there is always a temptation to think that the bits which finally resist his best efforts to understand them are the bits where the artist has failed. This would be true if one were the ideal reader. I think the poet will have failed in passages which continue to baffle the majority of attentive readers after the poem has been before the world for a century or so. But in each man's reading of a new poem his successes and failures in interpretation both depend so much on subjective and even momentary and accidental factors that no conclusion can be drawn.

From this difficult piece we turn to something more lyrical, more musical. The world is growing sharper, the focus harder. All its characters are soon to sink out of Logres into mere Britain or else to rise out of it into Carbonek. Crisis, in its etymological sense of Judgement, is at hand. The huge forces which came out of Broceliande to build Logres and remained to build Galahad, have done their work. Now they withdraw : it is *The Departure of Merlin*. He fades into the rich, fertile, dimness from which he came, leaving the world harder and brighter, better and worse, more redeemed and more condemned. We are here shown the sea-wood in two of its aspects. It is, on the one hand, the place where ' vigours of joy drive up ', where ' rich-ringed, young leaved, monstrous trunks rejoice '. But it is also, since it flows all round the world from Carbonek to P'o-Lu, the place where opposites meet. Williams does not mean that it is a place ' beyond good and evil ' : it is more a place *before* good and evil, a place of possibilities. The good man who goes there, by way of unchastened romantic love or what he would call ' nature-mysticism ', will be in danger of perdition. But the bad man who goes there by ' thinking with his blood ' or worshipping instinct or dabbling in the occult, may be in danger of salvation. He may, even there, reject it : he may, even in that dreaming silence, feel a hatred of good which does not relax. Hence, in this poem, the one sailor who 'leapt from the deck'. Williams's own note runs as follows : ' Those in the Antipodes (not formal Hell) even feel Broceliande ; they become aware of all moments beside the P'o-Lu one and . . . " hope springs eternal "—unless, like the one sailor, you really do hate the good. And the distance from the Antipodes is no greater, in Grace, than from, say, Camelot.'

This is a hard doctrine for rigid men and a dangerous one for soft men : yet I believe it to be true. Many of us perhaps, if all were known, by sinking away from the rational and ethical level, down into dream and impulse and the skirts of the unconscious, all lawless and amorphous within, surrendered like a floating leaf to all the currents of the ' sea-wood ', have found those seeds of good to which, under the Omnipotence, we now stand indebted for everything. Signposts to Paradise start up unexpectedly *vestibulum ante ipsum primis in faucibus Orci*. The danger of letting such a secret out is not very great if it is balanced by two warnings—first, that Carbonek lies only beyond ' *a certain part* of Broceliande ', and second, that Broceliande is not a short cut. You had much better go there *after* Byzantium. For if you go there first it is only seeds, only sign posts, that you will discover—if you even do that. And the sign post will point you back, back to the normal world ; and when you emerge into it everything will be still to do.

While Galahad sweeps on to the achievement of the Grail and Merlin ' fades away into the forest dim ' Palomides makes a good end. *The Death of Palomides* is a pale and quiet poem, in strong contrast to the richness and colour of the surrounding pieces. All those things which had agitated, for good or evil, the soul of the Saracen Knight, have fallen away from him. Iseult, fame, the Questing Beast, Dinadan—all that is over. These things had once appeared to him as ' stations ', places at which the soul could stop or in which she could even live. Now he knows that they were only paths : ' I know those terminable paths are only paths '—paths by which he has walked, wings on which he has flown, and which he feels rushing backward behind him as he approaches the end. His mind reverts not to any of these but to two old Levites whom he had once heard singing 'in a lodging of ancient Israel'. Their chant 'poured into channelled names' in formulae whose pure monotheism was a denial of the 'mathematics of Ispahan' (Dualism). One formula keeps on recurring to his memory—'The Lord created all things by means of his Blessing.' That is, for Palomides, all that now needs to be said, all that can be said. All that we have passed through, all that we have even rightly rejected, was created by the Blessing. For others, such as Galahad, the Faith may demand more complex and vibrant expression : but, if this will do, 'if this is the kingdom, the power, the glory', then Palomides' heart 'Formally offers the kingdom, endures the power'.

The title of the next poem, *Percivale at Carbonek*, is explained by the fact that Percivale is throughout the speaker ; the *subject* is Galahad at Carbonek. We are not yet at the climax of the story : that will come when Galahad sails to Sarras. But here, where he enters the 'spiritual place', heals the wounded king, and achieves the Grail, we are certainly at a preliminary climax : and Williams, in a certain sense, declines it. The glory of Carbonek and of the achievement is presented almost entirely in reverse and by implication during eleven stanzas which show Galahad kneeling in sorrow at the threshold of Carbonek ; kneeling, in fact, at that very gate where Lancelot had come slavering for his blood, a were-wolf. There are, I think, three reasons for this. The first is the obvious one, that the real climax of the cycle is coming later and this passage must be keyed down in proportion. The second, scarcely less obvious, is that many things in poetry affect us more if they are merely implied, as the greatness of Galahad's entry into Carbonek is implied by the still intensity with which the very angels, the 'scions of unremitted beauty' wait for Galahad to move. The third reason is the most important. Here, at the very frontier between Nature and Supernature, the threshold of Carbonek, Williams wants to exhibit to us something about which sacred poets are usually silent.

' Pascal ', said Williams, ' like all believers was a public danger '
(*Descent of the Dove*, p. 199). That is the sort of thing that has
often been said, and hotly, from outside, by unbelievers : the
admission from within is the novelty. Williams does not mean
in the least that believers are a danger in so far as they are unsatis-
factory believers who mistake the passions of the natural man in
them for zeal or his stupidities for guidance. That would, no
doubt, be true, but it is not the point that he is making. He
means that the saints, beginning with Christ Himself, not by
failure but by their very sanctity, inevitably cause immense
suffering. Christians naturally think more often of what the
world has inflicted on the saints ; but the saints also inflict much
on the world. Mixed with the cry of martyrs, the cry of nature
wounded by Grace also ascends—and presumably to heaven.
That cry has indeed been legitimized for all believers by the
words of the Virgin Mother herself—' Son, why hast thou thus
dealt with us ? Behold, thy father and I have sought thee
sorrowing.'

To be silent on this point was impossible for Williams. Even
if the relations of Galahad and Lancelot as he met them in Malory
had not invited the treatment of it, I think his own vision would
have forced him to treat it. He had no belief in a conception
of Grace which simply abolishes nature ; and he felt that there
was always something legitimate in the protests of nature against
the harrowing operation of conversion. This does not mean
that he wavered at all in his allegiance to that ' total pattern '
or glory which demands the harrowing. Rather, I think, he
felt that the final reconciliation, far from excluding, pre-supposed,
a full recognition of all that had been valid in the protests. It
was, after all, the protesting Job who had been accepted of God,
not the plausible comforters. His irony, his scepticism, his
pessimism must all be allowed their say. He was sure they were
not merely wrong. At the very least, he felt, Grace owes courtesy
to the Nature it so often must reject. The idea is expressed
whimsically in *The Descent of the Dove* where he says of St. John
of the Cross ' even he towards the end was encouraged to

remember that he liked asparagus ; our Lord the Spirit is reluctant to allow either of the two great Ways to flourish without some courtesy to the other'. It is expressed more gravely, but not yet tragically, in the poem on the *Death of Virgil*. There, it will be remembered, the redeemed souls who ran to rescue the great poet almost apologized to him for doing so. The order in which he was greater than they is not in the least abolished, even though at that moment it is manifestly transcended, by the order in which they are greater than he. On that level a happy and even frolic courtesy is all that is needed to resolve the tension. But at the gate of Carbonek it is different.

Galahad has caused Lancelot immense sorrow merely by being born. He has caused Lancelot (and the Round Table in general) further sorrow by beginning ' the adventures of the Sangreal', for 'when this rich thing goeth about the Round Table shall be destroyed'. His example has led many of them to undertake the quest of the Grail, and for them the quest has ended in humiliation and failure. This is ' the double misery' of Logres—to see their lower good destroyed by the higher and then to lose the higher also. Galahad has gained all : Lancelot seemingly has lost all, Lancelot by whom Galahad exists. And that is why at the gate of Carbonek ' Joy remembered joylessness : joy kneeled '. For nine stanzas Galahad implores pardon of his earthly father Lancelot—pardon for his very existence, forgiveness for ' the means of grace and the hope of glory'. Then, in one short stanza packed with movement the great act is begun and the poem ends with the formula (unconsciously but happily reminiscent of Beowulf's *Heorot is gefælsod*) ' Carbonek was entered '.

The problem presented in this passage is one of every day occurrence. Again and again the man who follows the new way must feel not only pity but even, in some curious sense, shame and guilt, before those on the old way whom he has troubled by so doing. Who can seek the Grail without damaging the Round Table ? (' Son, why hast thou thus dealt with us ? '). The tragic unity of Man decrees that the sanctification of each should be costly not only to Christ, not only to his fellow

Christians, but, more bewilderingly, to those whose shattered
parental ambition or wounded natural affection reproach him
with dumb pain and total misunderstanding—Son, why hast
thou thus dealt with us ?   Here it is resolved—in the only sense
in which such problems can be resolved—in the person of
Galahad.   However illogical such quasi-shame and quasi-guilt
may be, however dangerous to those whose feet are insecurely
set on the new way, they are, it seems, to be accepted.   And with
the acceptance the whole situation is altered.   Galahad's action
releases an old inhibition in our minds.   I do not know any other
poet who could have conceived this scene.   There are certain
depths of pathos which come only to those who abstain from the
more obvious and, as we say, the ' more human ' forms.

Between this poem and the *Last Voyage* we should probably
place *The Meditation of Mordred*.   The doom of Logres is almost
accomplished.   Gawaine, the king's nephew, son of Morgause
and Lot, whom Williams calls ' canonical Gawaine ' because the
canon or code of earthly honour is his only principle, urged on
by his half-brother Mordred, has revealed to Arthur the loves of
Guinivere and Lancelot.   The Table is rent.   There is civil war
between Lancelot's party and the King's.   Arthur is overseas
besieging Lancelot in his own kingdom of Benwick, ignoring
the letters in which the Pope urged him to make peace.   He has
left Mordred regent in his absence.   The poem is more completely dramatic, and simpler, than any other in the cycle.
Here, at last, after all the complex mythical figures which have
dominated the rest of the poem, we get a familiar human type :
naturally, for Logres is becoming Britain.   The bright cloud
which had almost descended to earth is being drawn back into
the Land of the Trinity whence it came : the hard, worldly,
unambiguous landscape emerges.   There is no irony in Mordred,
only commonplace cynicism.   He has, however, the poetic
dignity of being able to formulate his heart's desire.   He will
seize the kingdom and become a Western replica of the Emperor
of P'o-Lu.   For he knows that Byzantium is not the only
empire : there is another ' beyond miles of bamboo ' where ' a

small Emperor sits' among 'his tiny-footed, slant-eyed wives'.
Mordred thinks he will become like that—'I will have my
choice and be adored for the having.' In this picture of the
Antipodean Emperor there is a sickening combination of extreme
distance and extreme clarity. The whole poem is quiet. 'I
will sit here alone,' says Mordred. And 'here', which is
London and had once been Camelot, is now best defined as the
place from which Galahad and the Grail are rushing away.

That rushing movement is the predominant quality of *The
Last Voyage*. This does not mean that it has at all the kind of
rushing movement we find in Shelley—much less the galloping
movement of Swinburne. The idea of rapid and unimpeded
motion tends—or tended before the machine age—to be much
associated with freedom, loosening, relaxation, with broken
dams or horses 'given their heads'. What we have here is
something quite different. The motion is taut, vibrant : the
sense of quivering compulsion is behind it. The ship 'drove
into and clove the wind . . . swallowed in a path of power',
seizing 'the shortest way between points', fastened 'to the
right balance of the stresses', 'in a path of lineal necessity'.
Supporting this we have metallic, or at least mineral, images of
the figures on board it. Galahad in the prow is 'the alchemical
infant', Percival behind him a 'folded silver column', Bors
'mailed in black' ; for to us who live in the machine age images
of intense speed and power perhaps must be inorganic—we know
so many things stronger and swifter than animals. The birds,
which appear in the third paragraph are not here used as they
would probably have been in an earlier poet to suggest speed ;
that has already been done, and will be kept going by the refrain
'The ship of Solomon (blessed be he) drove on.' They are land
birds, doves, now 'sea travellers' because 'the land melts'.
According to Williams's note 'For them (i.e. Galahad and his
companions) all that was Logres and the Empire has become this
flight of doves. Galahad as a symbol of Christ now has necessity
of being in himself.'

The connexion between the first and the second sentence in

this note is not at first obvious. I think it is this. Until 'the necessity of being was communicated to the son of Lancelot', he was of course a derived being, indebted for existence not only to God but 'to Logres and the Empire', as you and I are dependent (if one inquires closely enough) on the whole of Nature. As he becomes Necessary Being, all that ceases to exist in its old relation to him. It is represented now only by the Doves, symbols of the Holy Ghost. Only as an expression of uncreated spirit does it now exist for him. And these birds, numerous as all the inhabitants of the empire (nay, they *are* 'the empire riding the skies of the ocean') 'overfeather' the whole ship lifting 'oak and elm to a new-ghosted power'. Thus, for the prose intellect. But the power of the symbol lies, I think, more in the simple idea that the solid land has become a flight of birds. It is this that makes us poetically believe that we are passing with all the speed of our 'arm-taut keel' beyond the phenomenal universe, through the 'everlasting spray of existence', the 'sea of omnipotent fact'; that we are witnessing apotheosis. But, as in all poetry that attempts such themes with success, so here, the symbolical miracles are braced with flashes of acute recollection from the sensuous world. Thus the line 'down the curved road among the topless waters' brings before us exactly what we have seen from real ships—not 'waves' coming towards us, nor even 'waves' rising and falling, but (as if stationary in that split second of sight) a terrible road down into a shining valley.

Three other pictures are let into the poem. First, before we see the ship of Solomon itself, we see the picture of that ship, and of other things, painted 'in the hall of empire'. Secondly, from the body of Dindrane lying in the ship, we turn aside to glance at the lady for whom Dindrane had died, dancing 'in the last candles of Logres'. The third flashes on us a glimpse of the savagery which now holds Britain. The murder of Dinadan by that fatal family 'the sons of the queen Morgause' is, however, not merely an instance of savagery. Brutal 'honour' and brutal treachery in league with one another 'are glad to destroy the pertinence of curiosity'. As the Moslem and the Manichaean from without close in to destroy, if they could, 'the golden Ambiguity' of the Incarnation, so the sons of Morgause destroy that other ambiguity, the good 'irony', the double vision of Dinadan. It is the triumph of Plain Man ; 'the lights are being put out all over Europe'.

In *The Prayers of the Pope* we are invited to study more fully this extinguishing of lights. The situation which 'the young Pope Deodatus, Egyptian-born' contemplates is of course very like that which Williams contemplated in 1944 and which we still contemplate in 1946. But the poem is not simply a tract for the times. We are seeing, partly, the real present ; partly the imaginary world of the poem ; partly the real past, the division of Christendom which culminated with the breach between Pope and Patriarch in 1054 and the great retreat of Christendom before Islam which had preceded it. More generally still, we are studying what is perhaps the most steadily recurrent of all historical phenomena. Again and again, if not the Grail and the Parousia, at least some great good almost descends to earth : again and again something arises which seems to be 'beyond history, holding history at bay' ; and each time the birth goes back, the sun, after one morning gleam, disappears. Every Logres fails to receive the Grail and sinks into a mere Britain : Israel, Athens, medieval Christendom, the Reformation, the Counter-Reformation, the Enlightenment. Nothing is further from the truth than the picture of history given in Keats's *Hyperion* where each perfection is ousted by 'a new perfection' treading on its heels. The movement is not from lovely Titans to still more lovely Gods, but from Augustus to Tiberius, from Arthur to Mordred, from Voltaire to Vichy—

> Mistletoe killing an oak,
> Rats gnawing cables in two,
> Moths making holes in a cloak—
> How they must love what they do !

From this spectacle, Williams's Pope does not draw absolute despair, but he offers no easy consolation. We must, it seems, reject from the outset the idea that since *Alles vergangliches ist nur ein gleichnis*, since every earthly good is only an image, therefore the breaking of that image ' doesn't matter '. It is only an image,

> ' But each loss of each image
> Is single and full, a thing unrequited,
> Plighted in presence to no recompense. '

Its loss leaves us ' rich in sorrow ' (hence the refrain ' Send not, send not the rich empty away ') and ' laden with loss '. And in so far as we feel ' loss ' we are affirming the lost image. The most willing and submissive acceptance of loss does that equally with the most sullen and reluctant : for if we deny the image we are losing, then clearly there is no loss to be accepted. (Muddle-headed characters in Elizabethan plays sometimes nobly reconcile themselves to death on the ground that life has never been worth having : but if so, there is no nobility in dying and nothing to be reconciled to.) The acceptance of loss therefore combines in itself the two ' Ways ', the Romantic and the Ascetic, the Affirmation and the Rejection of images. We affirm the image at the very moment of affirming its opposite. This is an ambivalence which ' our wit ', human consciousness, carries. But the archtype of it is an ambivalence which from the nature of things only the incarnate God can carry. By that *kenosis* wherein He willingly empties Himself of His glory to become Man, He at once affirms and rejects, not an image, but His very self. He affirms His uncreated glory ; to suppose that He belittles that as the muddled Elizabethan heroes belittle life would be to make Deity blaspheme Deity. He also affirms its opposite—the cradle at Bethlehem and the jeering in the Praetorium. Whatever the last word about all sacrifice and all the recurrent wrongs of history is going to be, it is not going to be Stoical. The sacrificed goods and the goods that perished were real goods : and God, so far from agreeing with Job's comforters, restored to Job just such ' images ' as he had lost ; ' fourteen thousand sheep, and six thousand camels, and a thousand yoke of oxen, and a thousand she asses, . . . seven sons and three daughters, . . . and in all the land were no women found so fair as the daughters of Job.' That is why the Pope prays

> O Blessed, confirm
> not thee in thine images only but thine images in thee.

The maxim ' Neither is this thou ' must not be allowed to oust its complement ' This also is thou '. The heart's desire, after all submission has been made and all patience practised, is rightly for ' the double inseparable wonder '—a Logres, a civilization, a Church which really affirm God, but also, which He really affirms.

In the meantime the promise of such a condition has been frustrated. All over the world the principle of co-inherence is lost. The true doctrine that

> the everlasting house the soul discovers
> is always another's,

has become hateful to men and they are ' frantic with fear of losing themselves in others ' so that they live at best for personal not for ' communicated ' glory and become ' puppets of reputation '. One result of this is that they are busily engaged in ' choosing foes '. For if one will not have the City one is driven by the necessity of one's nature to invent a substitute for it, and this cannot be done without finding a scapegoat. When race is separated from race ' and grace prized in schism ', when all our pleasure is to be *inside* some partial and arbitrary group, then of course, we must have ' outsiders ' to despise and denounce— Jews, Capitalists, Papists, the Bourgeoisie, what-not—or it is no fun. That is how ' the primal curse ' appears on the political level. For that primal curse is, for Williams, the refusal or denial of the Identity, the spirit which said in Eden ' Let us gaze, son of man, on the Acts in contention.' Of the same nature is the ' old necromantic gnosis '—all Gnostic, Manichaean, Nestorian, or Islamic heresies which deny the co-inherence of Deity and flesh in Christ.

This division, ' the miserable conquest of the categories over

identity' is not only the source of death ; death itself is such a
schism. In it the different 'themes' of Man fall apart and
become each merely itself : that is what we call decay. And so
also in spiritual death, this side the grave, the members become
'dreadfully autonomous'. This happens to some degree in
every fallen man : as he prays the Pope feels the horrible dis-
integration within him.

But if co-inherence is the one grand secret how can the faithful
remnant reject even the 'puppets of reputation' and 'evil
wizards' without committing the same sin as they ? As the
Pope says 'causes and catapults' are found on both sides of the
line, and so is 'the death of a brave beauty'. The difference
lies, and must always be made to lie, only in this, that we confess
and declare our co-inherence in them while they deny their
co-inherence in us. Wherever the true Church forgets this—as
she has repeatedly, almost continually done—she becomes herself
only one more of the sects, another 'dreadfully autonomous'
theme. No possible horror in the actions of the barbarians alters
this. Thus, at the very moment when the Pope reaffirms the
co-inherence the barbarian wizards are dragging from old graves
'the poor, long dead, long buried, decomposing shapes of
humanity', and it is an army of such 'mechanized bodies'
which makes the vanguard of the heathen hordes and whose
'cold coming' makes the consuls and lords of the empire shrink.
No matter : we are in the enemy and he in us.

So far we have had only the 'full glance at the worst'. Two
elements of hope now appear. Though Logres has fallen and
though all the Empire is now falling, Taliessin's household
remains. At the last hour he formally dissolves the Company,
while also declaring that the Company is 'still fixed in the will
of all who serve the Company'. That is, he 'restores to God the
once permitted lieutenancy', but the thing itself will go on.
Secretly, unknown to one another, far divided, little groups or
pairs of those who still follow the Way of Exchange will continue to exist amidst the wreck of the falling Empire. This is a
historical truth no less important than the truth that every

Logres sinks to a Britain. There is always something left, a 'remnant', a 'leaven', 'the Trojan few, the leavings of Achilles' spear'. Good is hard to preserve : but it is also terribly hard to eradicate completely. As Professor Powicke says, 'In all ages there have been civilized persons.' As Williams said to me in Addison's Walk, talking of the invasion of Norway, 'And yet, even there, at this moment, people are falling in love.' The great barbarian hordes go trampling past and 'stamp into darkness cities', but somehow something is left. This time Taliessin's work will be left : as Merlin had promised him at the very beginning. Those whose eyes are fixed on wide, general prospects might express the truth by saying that while every Logres fails some minor by-product of the original design usually survives. But then only the Emperor can say—and if the question should turn out to be meaningless even He cannot say—what is minor and what is major, which is the main design and which the by-product. In certain theologies the creation itself is a by-product of the fall of Lucifer and the Incarnation a by-product of the fall of man.

The second element of hope is harder to understand. In its literal sense the passage is easy enough. Galahad and his companions lie for a year and a day in a trance in Sarras. Meanwhile the giant tentacles of P'o-Lu feel their way along Burma, close to India. But there they meet an obstacle : something both like and unlike themselves meets them, holds them. The roots of Broceliande have fastened on them. Along all those miles of the submarine world the slimy tentacles of the Antipodes are 'tautened to Nimue's trees', 'fixed to a regimen' and 'held so forever'. And with that, all the death-forces begin to fail : even the Headless Emperor dissolves into a 'crimson tincture' on the waters. Galahad and his fellows stir and wake in the 'triple-toned light' of Sarras : and then

> The roses of the world bloomed from Burma to Logres ;
> pure and secure from the lost tentacles of P'o-l'u,[1]
> the women of Burma walked with the women of Caerleon.

[1] Williams was not consistent in his spelling of this name.

One explanation which might conceivably occur to a simple reader may be ruled out at once. This is not a ' poetic ' description of the Japanese advance on India and its failure. The whole of Williams's P'o-Lu was conceived, and (I think) this poem written before the Japanese entered the war : his ' gift of prophecy ' therein was a common topic of raillery among us.

One of the basic conceptions used in this passage is undoubtedly that which we have already met in *The Departure of Merlin*— that of the curious connexion, even, in a sense, the affinity between the last evil and the first seminal principles as they exist in Nimue. Down on the ocean bed the tentacles of P'o-Lu and the roots of Broceliande are not far apart. Good is at least as deep rooted in the sub-world, as tenacious and omnivorous, as evil. If evil, the Headless Emperor, chooses to go down there, calls for the combat on that level, in the depths of the womb and in the instinctive dark, there also he will find his conqueror. But how or why something little short of a re-demption of the whole natural order (the roses of the world blooming from Burma to Logres) should occur at that moment, or how this is to be fitted into the chronology of the legend, I do not know. Perhaps the words ' a year and a day ' are ambigu-ous. Perhaps it is at the end of the world that the New Man wakes in Sarras and this whole passage is a prophecy of the great Restoration. But I end in doubts.

The cycle closes (in *Taliessin at Lancelot's Mass*) as Malory had closed with Lancelot contrite and entered into religion, and Guinevere made nun at Almesbury. All has been forgiven and all has been exchanged. The substitution of Elayne for Guine-vere long since in Lancelot's bed has led, in Galahad, to the healing of the Wounded King. Arthur and Pelles exchange functions as Lancelot celebrates mass. The dead Knights are all invisibly present and adore. Here, out of time, the universal reconciliation hinted in the previous poem, is actual. The ' white rushing deck ' of Solomon's ship retrieves even ' the antipodean zones '. Over the altar in a ' flame of anatomized fire ' there appears either Galahad in Christ or Christ manifested in His image Galahad.   He is the porphyry stair, the ascent to the vision of the Emperor.   All that Logres has been, all that it eternally is at its ' climax tranquil in Venus ', adores, ' each in turn lordliest and least ' : for the order is at once ' hierarchic and republican ', not flat equality but a whirling carnival of interchanged dominion and service.   The ' unseen knight of terror ' remains cryptic because we lack the poems which Williams intended to write about him.   For the rest there is, I think, nothing in this piece which requires explanation ; its only mysteries are those of poetry itself and of its high matter. The last stanza returns us strongly and gently to the real world. ' That which was once Taliessin '—we may now almost read ' which was once Charles Williams ' rides away, out of sight— ' Let the Company pray for it still.'

VI

Conclusions

So far I have been trying to explain rather than to judge. In this last chapter I shall put forward a few guesses as to the permanent place of this poem in English literature. More than guesses they cannot be. The history of a poem is only beginning when it is first printed. We cannot be sure that posterity will be any wiser than we, but they are not likely to be foolish in exactly the same ways. A work of art has to be seen in many different lights and to test itself against many different kinds of capacity and experience before it finds its level.

Obviously by far the greatest danger of extinction which threatens this poem will come from its obscurity. And that danger will probably increase with time : not because the poem itself will become harder—it may, for a very considerable time, become easier—but because the extreme indulgence towards obscurity which characterizes the taste of modern readers is not very likely to last. The critics who are now in their cradles may well head a reaction ; a new Waller and a new Denham may arise : lucidity, even to excess, may be once more demanded, and all those whom we call Moderns be banished to the lumber room as speedily as the Augustans banished the Metaphysicals. For the moment all we can do is to distinguish between different kinds of obscurity, of which all at least ought not to militate equally against a poem's acceptance. I distinguish four kinds.

(1) Obscurity may come from mere slovenliness of syntax. Poets, as well as prose writers, may compose sentences which are difficult to ' construe '. This source of obscurity is insufficiently attended to. Our fathers got into a habit of talking as if all the difficulties in Browning were due to the subtlety of his thought. Recently, re-reading *The Ring and the Book* after an interval of about twenty years, I was astonished to find that in

nearly every instance the passages which gave me pause did so solely because I had misunderstood the construction. One was baffled not at the points where the poet had something unusually difficult to say but at those where he used injudiciously the English licence of omitting the relative pronoun. A re-writing which removed ninety-nine per cent of the difficulties would have left all the philosophical and psychological niceties intact. Obscurity of this kind is simply a vice. And it certainly does occur in Williams. Thus the line ' who fly the porphyry stair ' is intended to mean ' who fly up the porphyry stair '. But by the nature of the English language it cannot do so. This is a bad fault—and the poet bore with patience my perhaps over-violent condemnation of it. But the fault does not occur often. His fame will not shipwreck on that rock.

(2) Obscurity may be deliberate. No poetry worth the name can be perfectly translated into prose : but the poet may choose to write poetry which makes, not perfect translation but any translation, impossible. He may be studiously ambiguous as if to show the intellect that nothing is being offered to it and all to the emotions. This is legitimate, but does not much concern us here. It is no commoner in Williams than in most poets ; less common, perhaps, than in many of his contemporaries

(3) ' Privatism '. This occurs when the poet writes what the reader, however sensitive and generally cultivated he may be, could not possibly understand unless the poet chose to tell him something more than he has told. Thus I was informed that I had been wasting my time trying to puzzle out certain lines in a modern poet because the real explanation lay not in the poems but in certain events that had happened while the poet was spending a week-end in my informant's house. In so far as the poem was addressed to a circle of friends such ' privatism ' is not a literary fault at all : in so far as the poem was exposed without warning for sale in the shops it seems to me to be simply a way of ' obtaining money under false pretences '. If I do not desire a law against this form of cheating, that is only because such a law would be too difficult either to frame or to administer. The

thing involves such a blend of dishonesty, puerility, and dis-
courtesy, such a denial of 'Co-inherence', such a reckless under-
mining of the very conditions in which literature can flourish,
that no punishment which criticism can inflict could be sufficiently severe. Yet as every casuist knows wicked acts and
innocent ones may have smudgy frontiers. Where usury begins
and co-operation ends, where killing in war becomes murder,
where punishment becomes revenge—there are hard questions.
We must therefore admit that 'Privatism' is not always easily
distinguished from what I am going to call 'Unshared Background'.

(4) An example of difficulties arising from Unshared Background would be *The Waste Land*. If you have never read
Dante or Shakespeare certain things in that poem will be obscure
to you. But then, frankly, we ought to have read Dante and
Shakespeare ; or at least the poet has a right to address only
those who have done so. And if the only result of a first reading
of *The Waste Land* were to send you to Dante and Shakespeare,
your time and money would have been very well spent. Similarly in Williams. He assumes that you know the Bible, Malory,
and Wordsworth pretty well, and that you have at least some
knowledge of Milton, Dante, Gibbon, the *Mabinogion*, and
Church history. Difficulties of this sort are wholly legitimate.
But there are border-line cases. When Mr. Eliot assumes that
you know Miss Weston's *From Ritual to Romance*, or Williams
that you know Heracleitus as quoted by W. B. Yeats—or still
more when the one assumes a knowledge of the Tarot pack and
the other of the Sephirotic Tree—the difficulties are becoming
less obviously legitimate. We have not, indeed, reached the
frontiers of vicious Privatism. The things referred to are
accessible : the poet may be innocently mistaken about the
extent to which they are—still more about the extent to which
they ought to be—matters of common knowledge among
educated people. (The value of Miss Weston's work is, for
example, a matter of controversy.) To refer to them is not the
same sort of thing as to sell to all a poem which will work only

for those who know the colour of your nurse's hair, the jokes of your preparatory school, or the favourite sayings of your aunt's parrot. Yet it is obvious that there will come a point at which you use in your poetry scraps of your own reading so intrinsically unimportant and so very unlikely to be shared by the best readers, that you have become guilty of Privatism. I am confident that Williams never intentionally crossed that line : and I am not certain of any passage where he crosses it in fact.

Supposing, then, that the obscurity does not succeed in killing the poem (and to dissipate that obscurity is the purpose of this book) we may proceed to consider its positive qualities. Lists of the demands which a great poem must fulfil are, of course, arbitrary : and if I here advance one it is mainly as a convenient way of bringing ' my discourse into frame '.

Firstly, then, after all that is come and gone, I think we demand of a great poem something that can be called Wisdom. We wish, after reading it to understand things in general, or at least some things, better than we did before. Wisdom by itself does not make a great poem or even a poem at all : and the value of a poem is by no means in direct ratio to its wisdom. But the demand for wisdom remains. It is indeed so strong that critics to whom the obvious content of an old poet is mere ' theological rubbish ' usually find it necessary to convince themselves that he had some profound wisdom of quite a different kind, some ' real subject ' which no generation till our own ever suspected. The whole biographical bias of modern (or recent) criticism is possibly due to the desire to find wisdom in poems whereof the obvious meaning has ceased to appear wise. If Heaven and Hell, gods and heroes, the innocence of Imogen and the horrors of conscience in *Macbeth*, seem to a man ' rubbish ', then his last resource for restoring importance to the texts is to suppose that the poet is revealing the secrets of his own heart. The demand that to read great verse should be to grow in wisdom has not really altered.

Secondly, we demand what I should call Deliciousness—what the older critics often called simply ' Beauty '. The poem must please the senses, directly by its rhythms and phonetic texture, indirectly by its images. It must no doubt do other things as well : harsh lines and dreadful or ugly images will have their place. But where there is no deliciousness in a long work there will be no poem.

Thirdly we demand what I call Strength of Incantation. The imagined world of the poem must have a consistency and vitality which lay hold of the mind. It must not be left to *us* to keep it going. It should be difficult for us to escape from it. It should remain with us as a stubborn memory like some real place where we have once lived—a real place with its characteristic smells, sounds, and colours : its unmistakable, and irreplaceable ' tang '. (This solidity and unmistakableness does not prove a poem great, for a bad poem may also be ' a world of its own ' ; Tupper is a distinctive country of the mind. But the absence of this quality is fatal.)

I begin then by considering these *Arthuriana* as a book of wisdom—a book that makes consciousness. If I say that in this respect it seems to me unequalled in modern imaginative literature, I am not merely recording the fact that many of Williams's doctrines appear to me to be true. I mean rather that he has re-stated to my imagination the very questions to which the doctrines are answers. Whatever truths or errors I come to hold hereafter, they will never be quite so abstract and jejune, so ignorant of relevant data, as they would have been before I read him. Thus a good many debates one has heard between Romantics and Counter-Romantics become simply out of date as soon as one has grasped that ' Carbonek is beyond *a certain part* of Broceliande '. In the same way a good deal of what one has heard (and, alas, said) about sensual and super-sensual elements in love is, not so much refuted, as simply superseded by his whole conception of the body, his insistence that to reject carnal fruition is not to turn away from the body. Indeed this poet even where he celebrates abstinence—or there most—makes us feel that we have never *attended* to the body before. Perhaps the distinction between ' wisdom ' and simple knowledge comes out best in connexion with his more explicitly religious symbols. These, of course, cannot by a non-Christian reader be credited with the same kind of 'truth' which a Christian reader finds in them. Yet both readers will grow in Wisdom by contemplating them. The different forms under which the Divine appears—dim Carbonek, hierarchical Byzantium, ' climax tranquil in Venus ', and Deep Heaven opening beyond Jupiter—are new light on the nature of that Reality (if it be a reality) or on the nature of that illusion (if it be an illusion). To the militantly anti-Christian reader they are indeed most valuable information. What is the good of spending your whole energy in attacking Byzantium (as so many Atheists do) if all the time, unsuspected in the far west, Carbonek has been at least equally central to your enemy's position ?

Consider, again, how in the matter of irony Williams begins where nearly every modern writer leaves off. No age has been more ironical than ours : irony has even been made by some critics into a necessary element of all poetry To that extent Williams is a child of his age. But that kind of irony at which others arrive on their final goal is for him the starting-point. It is for him what you get over almost before beginning to write. The true goal is ' defeated irony ' : and it makes the lower irony (to me) look simply stupid—' swainish ' as Milton would have said. The work of Lytton Strachey, read immediately after Williams's poetry, would, I suspect, sound pitiable. To Strachey, laboriously picking out every admission, every scrap of correspondence wrenched from its context, which can make it appear that his eminent Victorians were really very absurd people, the spirit of defeated irony replies ' But *of course* ! ' Who ever supposed otherwise ? Of course all great men, all men, are absurd. And now let us begin the rite of honouring these eminent Victorians. Let us run to succour their falling as we did to succour Virgil in his fall ! And against that Strachey's work sounds like the heavy flop of a large man who has tried to dive and failed. We can only hasten with all possible courtesy to rescue him also. He has not been ironical enough.

Conclusions

Other modern myths depict a dialectical world. Keats's Titans and Wagner's Gods beget their opposites and are transcended by them. Williams paints a Co-inherent world : 'joy remembers joylessness'. If this is a truth at all it is certainly a more interesting and subtle truth, and a fresher, if not a newer, one.

In other writers we take the good' characters for granted and explain the bad ones. Richard is bad because he is deformed, Edmund because he is a bastard. In Williams we explain the good ones. A good character is for him one who *has become* good. This was so already in his novels. Hence of Sybil in *The Greater Trumps* and her blessed state of mind we are told that it

'had not been easily reached. That sovereign estate, the inalienable heritage of man, had been in her, as in all, falsely mortgaged to the intruding control of her own greedy desires. Even when the true law had been discovered, when she knew that she had the right and the power to possess all things, on the one condition that she herself was possessed, even then her freedom to yield herself had been won by many conflicts.'

So in the poem,

> many a mile of distance in the Empire was to go
> to the learning, many a turn of exchange.

We see Taliessin learning, and afterwards we see the slaves learning in his household. This also appears to me to be ' wise ' : I do not mean, of course, that the poem is a poem of ' characters ' as an epic or drama might be. Character is not there for its own sake, and what is there is stylized and limited for symbolic and lyric purposes. The wonder is that, despite this self-limitation, so much merely personal tragedy and even social comedy is interwoven with the myth. The persons are not abstractions. There is more merely human life in them than the poet, for his main purpose, needed to show. It gets out, it is irrepressible.

In ' Wisdom ' then I believe the work abounds and even excels. Next for Deliciousness, and first for Deliciousness of

rhythm and melody. This is the quality in which I consider the
work most unequal—at least as posterity will read it. His own
incantatory powers were very great and no line that he wrote did
not sound musical when he recited it. But that is an advantage
which, I suppose, many poets have had and which all must lose
at death. We can judge the poetry only as read without it.
Metrically the individual poems fall into two classes : those in
rhyming or unrhyming stanzas and those in continuous five-
beat verse (with occasional internal rhyme). It is in the latter
that the poet seems to me, at times, to falter. He is using Sprung
Rhythm in which a single syllable may be a foot. This technique
at its best can fling stressed monosyllables together so as to
produce an unsurpassed weight and resonance. Thus in the
crushing lyric of Lamorack and Morgause,

> Her hand discharged catastrophe. I was thrown
> before it. I saw the source of all stone.

Or, with a less catastrophic effect, but sharp as a cracked whip

> Taliessin's voice sharpen'd
> On Virgil's exact word.

Or stealthily,

> Feeling along Burma, nearing India.

But in the longer and less lyrical pieces (which contain nearly
all the inferior work) it seems to me to be used at times with no
justification either in the emotional context or in the resulting
rhythm. I find no beauty in such lines as

> This, fable or truth, none knew

or

> over his tunic : laced boots of hide,

where the rhythm forces those boots into a prominence which
they never do anything to deserve. On the other hand there
are poems in which Williams has produced word music equalled

by only two or three in this century and surpassed by none. *The Calling of Arthur* responds metrically to every movement of the emotion : startling and shrill in its opening stanza (' Black with hair, bleak with hunger, defiled '), dragging and fainting for King Cradlemas (' The high aged voice squeals with callous comfort '), rising into a rapid and more familiar rhythm as action begins (' The banner of Bors is abroad ; where is the king ') and then, at the end, using all its monosyllabic feet and clashing accents to convey an astonishing sense of violent and conclusive action,—

> a screaming few
> fled : Merlin came : Camelot grew . . .

slowing into the full and stately finality of the sprung Alexandrine

> In Logres the King's friend landed, Lancelot of Gaul.

Less excited but even richer in pure sound is *The Crowning of Arthur*. Here a particularly fine effect is achieved by the long lines as they rise—one might almost say, as they *escape*—out of the mass of the shorter lines stiffened with heavy syllables and jewelled with internal rhymes. Thus in ' The King stood crowned ; around in the gate ' we ourselves stand rigid ; in the last line of the same stanza (' Logres heraldically flaunted the King's state ') that long waving word *heraldically* lifts us banner high above the crowd. Equally beautiful in their places are

> sidereally pointed, the lord Percivale

or

> in beleaguered Sophia they sang of the dolorous blow.

I say ' in their places ' for this last line, in isolation, would be only the jog-trot of English ' anapæsts '. It is one of Williams's idioms thus to take what in itself would be an obvious and light rhythm and so to place it that it carries over weight and subtlety from the preceding lines while yet retaining enough of its native lightness to give the feeling of liberation. Thus ' And the heart of our Lord Taliessin determined the war ' would be nothing by itself—apart from the use of 'determined'. Now hear it in its function—

> the paps of the day were golden girdled ;
> hair, bleached white by the mere stress of the glory,
> drew the battle through the air up threads of light.
> The Tor of Badon heard the analytical word ;
> the grand art mastered the thudding hammer of Thor,
> and the heart of our lord Taliessin determined the war.

The whole quality of *and the heart of our lord Taliessin* is altered by its rhythmical equivalence to *the grand art mastered* : and indeed by the pressure of the whole poem that precedes it.

The ear, then, must give this poem sometimes blame, sometimes the highest praise ; I turn to the more difficult subject of its imagery. It must be said at the outset that Williams does not abound in that kind of imagery which is the peculiar glory of older English poetry—the sharply recognisable picturing of familiar (usually rural) objects. His snow that 'falls over brick and prickle' (how admirably those objects are selected !), his 'curved road among the topless waters', and his 'rain-dark stones' are exceptions ; and even of those the topless waters belong to the 'sea of omnipotent fact' and the 'rain-dark stones' are the pupils of a man's eyes. I remember only one simile of the old type in the poem,

> as the south wind, stirring the tiny waves, shows
> and shakes the stillness of the wide accumulated air.

Where he is most visual he is usually dealing with something other than Nature. Thus as the slave raises the bucket from the well, 'a round plane of water rose shining in the sun ', or, again,

> he saw
> through the unshuttered openings of stairs and rooms
> the red flares of processional torches and candles
> winding to the king's bed,

or the fires of torches at Arthur's coronation 'pouring' amid 'burning mail'. But none of these illustrate his most characteristic use of the senses.

His characteristic use of the senses is difficult to define and can be best understood by a few examples. 'A star rode by through the round window in the sky of Camelot.' That can, of course, be pictured : but the picture by itself is not remarkable enough to explain the potency of the phrase. Everything depends on the words *sky of Camelot*. For Camelot is 'London-in-Logres', a spiritual place, a state of being, which cannot really be seen at all. That, if you will, is why it has its own 'sky' ; and placing that sky in the simple visual image of a round window the poet makes us seem to see the invisible. Similarly Taliessin's unicorn is ' the animal which is but a shade till it starts to run '. We have the impression that we have seen a picture, though on analysis it turns out that the thing is not really picturable. In the same way ' a trumpet's sound ' can ' leap level with the arm ' of the slave who is carrying a bucket of water : the noise ' round with breath ' as the arm is round with flesh : the esemplastic power fuses together images from different senses and uses them, thus fused, to suggest the quite supersensible ' straightness ' which is one of the main themes of the whole poem. One might almost say that as Williams is the poet of ' defeated irony ' so he is the poet of the ' defeated senses ', or rather of the transmuted senses, of poetry which by an unfulfilled invitation to the senses lures us beyond them ; his poetical city ' is built at the meeting place of substance and sensuality '. He is in one way full of images : but where he is most himself each image is no sooner suggested than it fades—or, dare I say ? *brightens*—into something invisible and intangible. Such are Morgause's ' hewn eyelids ' ; the ' horizon ' in a girl's eyes ' breaking with distant Byzantium ' ; ' the height of the thin night air of Quinquagesima ' ; ' a storm of violent kings ' ; or best of all for our purpose since it is not only an instance but also a description of his poetic method, the city of Sarras

> on a sea-site
> in a light that shone from behind the sun.

One way of bringing out this quality in Williams's poetry would be to contrast it with two other kinds of poetry. Thus, on the one hand, it is obviously different from the fully and strictly visual poetry of Milton's ' chequered shade ' or Tennyson's ' wrinkled sea '. On the other hand it is equally different from Donne's ' stiff twin compasses ' or Mr. Eliot's ' patient etherized upon a table ' ; it has not that preference for what is harsh and superficially ' unpoetical '. Rather, it has a foot in both worlds. It uses the ' romantic ' images in the ' metaphysical ' way. The continual quiver of the aroused, yet transcended, senses (like his own ' infinitesimal trembling of the roses ') makes the very texture of his writing. It is all ' stuff of Caucasia fashioned in Byzantium ' and ' everywhere the light through the great leaves is blown '.

This is one source of that ' strength of incantation ' in which, if I may judge by my own experience, the poem excels : and here I expect that even those who most dislike it will agree with me. I cannot imagine the reader who would condemn it (that is, sincerely condemn, for men can *say* anything) on the score that it did nothing much or was too like other poems he had read. Those who dislike it will, I think, confess that it has a very positive quality, a taste which, if you hate, you will find it difficult to get out of the mouth. The world of the poem is a strong, strange, and consistent world. If the poem is rejected you will reject it because you find that world repellent. And that is a reaction which, though I do not share it, I can understand. It is certainly not a world I feel at home in, any more than I feel at home in the worlds of Dante and Milton. It strikes me as a perilous world full of ecstasies and terrors, full of things that gleam and dart, lacking in quiet, empty spaces. Amid the ' surge and thunder ' of the *Odyssey* you can get a snug fireside night in Eumaeus's hut. There is no snugness in Williams's Arthuriad, just as there is none in the *Paradiso*. What quiet there is is only specious : the roses are always trembling, Broceliande astir, planets and emperors at work. Can we then condemn it, as Raleigh came near to condemning *Paradise Lost* because it was insufficiently homely ? Not, I think, unless we know that comfort and heartsease are characters so deeply rooted in the real universe that any poetic world which omits them is a distortion : an assurance which I, to my sorrow, lack. Perhaps the universe of *Taliessin* and *The Region* is quite as like the real universe as what we find in *Pickwick* or *Tristram Shandy*. What provides relaxation in it, and thus, in a sense, takes the place of snugness, is gaiety—a stranger to poetry for some hundreds of years, but certainly no stranger to the universe. I am speaking of the gaiety of Dinadan, of Taliessin himself, of the stripped maids frolicking in Caucasia, and of the high courtesy and defeated irony which runs about the whole poem. There is a youthfulness in all Williams's work which has nothing to do with immaturity. Nor is this the only respect in which his world offers the very qualities for which our age is starved. Another such quality is splendour : his world is one of pomp and ritual, of strong, roaring, and resonant music. The transparent water-colour effect of much *vers libre* is not found there. His colours are opaque : not like stained glass but like enamel. Hence his admirable hardness ; by which I do not here mean difficulty, but hardness as of metals, jewels, logic, duty, vocation. Eroticism, in some form or other, is not a quality in which modern literature is deficient : but the pervasive eroticism—the glowing, pungent, aromatic quality—of these poems is different, and possible only to a poet who also appreciates austerity. Side by side with the splendour and the erotic perfume we meet celibacy, fasts, vigils, contrition, tragedy, and all but despair. This balance is true to the poet's originals : and that truth also contributes to the strength of the incantation. It is an advantage which few re-fashioners of old myths have had. All through *The Ring* the original Nibelungen story is pulling against the political and economic stuff with which Wagner wants to load it : all through Tennyson's *Idylls* the Arthurian story is pulling against nearly everything that Tennyson wants to say. There is no such tension in William's Arthuriad. It is in one way a wholly modern work, but it has grown spontaneously out of Malory and if the king and the Grail and the begetting of Galahad still serve, and serve perfectly, to carry the twentieth-century poet's meaning, that is because he has penetrated more deeply than the old writers themselves into what they also, half consciously, meant and found its significance unchangeable as long as there remains on earth any attempt to unite Christianity and civilization.